SAKI

Saki (H. H. Munro)

Original and Uncollected Stories

Edited, annotated and introduced by
Bruce Gaston

https://www.openbookpublishers.com
Notes and Introduction ©2024 Bruce Gaston. Original stories by 'Saki' (H. H. Munro).

This work is licensed under an Attribution-NonCommercial 4.0 International (CC BY-NC 4.0). This license allows you to share, copy, distribute and transmit the text; to adapt the text for non-commercial purposes of the text providing attribution is made to the authors (but not in any way that suggests that they endorse you or your use of the work). Attribution should include the following information:

Bruce Gaston, *Saki (H. H. Munro): Original and Uncollected Stories*. Cambridge, UK: Open Book Publishers, 2024, https://doi.org/10.11647/OBP.0365

Further details about CC BY-NC licenses are available at
http://creativecommons.org/licenses/by-nc/4.0/

All external links were active at the time of publication unless otherwise stated and have been archived via the Internet Archive Wayback Machine at https://archive.org/web

Any digital material and resources associated with this volume may be available at https://doi.org/10.11647/OBP.0365#resources

ISBN Paperback: 978-1-80511-141-2
ISBN Hardback: 978-1-80511-142-9
ISBN Digital (PDF): 978-1-80511-143-6
ISBN Digital eBook (EPUB): 978-1-80511-144-3
ISBN XML: 978-1-80511-146-7
ISBN HTML: 978-1-80511-147-4

DOI: 10.11647/OBP.0381

Cover illustration: Postcard LL3612, the Leonard A. Lauder collection of Raphael Tuck & Sons postcards, Curt Teich Postcard Archives Collection, The Newberry Library.
Cover design: Jeevanjot Kaur Nagpal

Contents

Introduction	1
Chronology	11
Esmé	15
Tobermory	21
Mrs. Packletide's Tiger	29
The Background	33
The Jesting of Arlington Stringham	37
Adrian	41
The Chaplet	47
Wratislav	51
Filboid Studge	55
Ministers of Grace	59
Mrs. Pendercoet's Lost Identity	67
The Optimist	71
The Romance of Business	77
Further Reading	79
Textual Variants	83

Introduction[1]

This book reprints—for the first time in over a hundred years—thirteen stories originally published in newspapers and magazines by Hector Hugh Munro, otherwise known as 'Saki'. Three of these ('Mrs. Pendercoet's Lost Identity', 'The Romance of Business' and 'The Optimist') are stories that have so far been missed by anthologists and editors. The other ten may seem familiar at first sight, but in fact are earlier—and, I would argue, better—versions of tales that later appeared in book form, first in the volume *The Chronicles of Clovis* and later in various "Collected" editions. In fact, few critics and even fewer readers are aware of the existence of these alternative versions.

Explaining why the stories ended up being rewritten requires some contextualisation. On 15 February 1911, Munro sent a letter to the publisher John Lane, owner of The Bodley Head: "I am sending you some of my collected sketches which you might like to publish in volume form. Methuen have published two previous books of mine, but they are dreadfully un-enterprising in the way of advertising" (Gibson 223, letter #1).[2]

Munro was referring here to *Reginald* (1904) and *Reginald in Russia* (1910), which reprinted stories published between 1901 and 1909, almost all of them in the *Westminster Gazette*. Writing for newspapers had been Munro's principal source of income ever since 1900, when the *Westminster Gazette* printed a series of political satires he had written inspired by *Alice in Wonderland*. These were so successful that they

---

[1] This introduction is derived in part from an article published in *ANQ: A Quarterly Journal of Short Articles, Notes and Reviews*, October 2021, copyright Taylor & Francis, https://doi.org/10.1080/0895769X.2021.1979929

[2] I am quoting the letters from Gibson 2014. The originals are archived at the Harry Ransom Humanities Research Center at the University of Texas. For a fuller discussion of Munro's business letters, see Frost 2001.

were then collected in book form as *The Westminster Alice* (1902). With remarkable ease and speed Munro turned out journalism, short stories, political satires, humorous verse, one-act plays, and parliamentary sketches. He found a ready market, for literacy rates had risen steeply over the previous few decades, and there had been a corresponding growth in the number of newspapers, magazines and periodicals. Short stories—a relatively new genre—had developed in tandem with these societal changes and were perfectly fitted to the new media.

Lane's reply to Munro's inquiry has not survived but it must have been favourable since Munro then sent him a list of thirteen stories, all published since 1909, which could be included in the planned book. This letter also proposed a title: *Tobermory and Other Sketches*. Another letter followed on 26 April 1911, adding four recently published stories ('The Easter Egg', 'The Chaplet', 'The Peace of Mowsle Barton' and 'Mrs. Packletide's Tiger').[3] Perhaps aware that "[w]hile miscellaneity could be a selling point for periodicals, it was generally the opposite for books" (Zacks 14), Munro offered some suggestions for a general theme and a title: "Four or five of the stories deal prominently with animals, and perhaps 'Beasts and Super Beasts' [sic] would be a better title than 'Tobermory'" (Gibson 224, letter #3). In fact, the collection ended up being called *The Chronicles of Clovis* and Munro had to keep "Beasts and Super-Beasts" for his subsequent book (1914), which did indeed contain a good number of stories featuring animals.

Just like the short story itself, book-length collections of short stories were a relatively new development. From the author's point of view, reprinting short stories in book form was a useful way of getting paid a second time for the same work (Baldwin 95). For the publisher, on the other hand, there was the problem that a short-story collection would have to compete against novels in the bookshops and lending libraries. The latter genre had the advantage of being longer established and consequently enjoying more respectability and popularity. Moreover, an axiom developed early among publishers (and persists to the present day) that books of short stories do not sell as well as novels (Lewis 115–16; Baldwin 99). Ever since Dickens many short-story authors had

---

3   A full list of dates and places of publication of all Munro's stories can be found at https://www.annotated-saki.info/first-publication.

attempted to blur the lines between a novel and a short-story collection by using some kind of framing narrative or other device to give unity to what would otherwise be a series of independent and unrelated tales (Lewis 57–70). These considerations doubtless played a role in the choice of a title for the volume that Munro and the Bodley Head were planning. Munro's first two books had a clear focus: *The Westminster Alice* collected his *Alice in Wonderland* parodies and the stories in *Reginald* are given a unity by having the eponymous dandy as either the main character or narrator. The follow-up, *Reginald in Russia*, has a title clearly chosen to recall the previous work but it is in fact a misnomer, as only the first story involves Reginald, who then vanishes from the Munro canon for ever. Presumably *The Chronicles of Clovis*, an alliterative title suggesting the episodic adventures of another young man, was intended to aid sales by reminding potential readers of the previous two collections.

The letters strongly imply that the new title was the publisher's idea, while Munro remained sceptical. Even when the book was released, he could not resist having a dig at it, writing in another letter to Lane: "Of course the sale is going to be damned by the title. An elderly gentleman told me he could not read French history of such a remote period" (Gibson 227, letter #11). He was referring to the fact that there had been four kings of the Franks named Clovis in the pre-medieval period. (On the other hand, it is open to doubt whether the "elderly gentleman" ever existed.) Nonetheless, Munro fell in with his publisher's wishes and in response began to reorient the planned volume away from animals and towards the incorrigible young man Clovis Sangrail, the protagonist of four stories written over the last two years ('The Match-Maker', 'The Stampeding of Lady Bastable' under its original title 'A Modern Boy', 'The Unrest-Cure' and 'The Quest'). Now that the title had been decided upon, he penned another four Clovis stories in as many months: first 'The Peace Offering' (see Gibson 224, letter #4), then 'A Matter of Sentiment', 'The Recessional' and 'The Talking-Out of Tarrington'.[4] After all, a book with "Clovis" in its title would necessarily have to feature that character prominently.

The second thing the new title prompted Munro to do was to

---

4 I am working on the assumption that Munro submitted his stories as soon as they were completed and that these were then swiftly printed. It would not have been in either his or the newspaper's interests to delay publication.

insert Clovis into some of the stories that had already been published in newspapers. In 'The Chaplet' and 'The Background', this was done through the simple expedient of adding a short narrative frame with Clovis as the narrator of the main story. Many writers have made use of this structure of a story-within-a-story, as it offers interesting possibilities in terms of characterisation, style of language, narrative voice and even unreliable narration. Munro, however, does not avail of these, and Clovis' presence is in no way essential, for all of Munro's humorous stories are narrated in what is essentially the same mannered and ironic style, no matter whether the narrator is an omniscient third-person one or a character such as Clovis, Reginald, or the Baroness (in 'Esmé'). In other stories, Munro has Clovis pop up for a sentence or two to make a facetious comment, then withdraw again (for example, in 'Mrs. Packletide's Tiger'). He is also sent far afield whenever the plot requires it, visiting the Swiss Alps in the company of Adrian and Mrs. Mebberley, and apparently getting to know Wratislav's family in Vienna. This last is a particularly clumsy example of these additions. The original begins: "The Gräfin's two elder sons had made deplorable marriages. It was a family habit". For *The Chronicles of Clovis* this became: "The Gräfin's two elder sons had made deplorable marriages. It was, observed Clovis, a family habit". There is no explanation of how Clovis has come to make this observation, nor do we know to whom it is addressed. He plays no further role in the story. This kind of thing is presumably what A.A. Milne was thinking of when he commented in his introduction for the 1926 uniform edition on how "Clovis exercises, *needlessly*, his titular right of entry" into 'The Background' and 'Mrs. Packletide's Tiger' (xiii, my emphasis).[5]

As a consequence of Munro's rewriting, *The Chronicles of Clovis* ended up containing twenty Clovis stories (out of a total of 28). This is a doubling of his participation compared to the originals.

The additions lead one to wonder whether Clovis was only added later as a narrator to two of the other stories in *The Chronicles of Clovis*. 'The Story of St. Vespaluus' and 'The Way to The Dairy' were not printed anywhere else before their inclusion in *The Chronicles of Clovis*, so the

---

[5] Milne may have known the originals: "It was in the *Westminster Gazette* that I discovered him" (*ibid.*).

question can never be answered definitively, but—just like with 'The Chaplet' and 'The Background'—their frame narratives are largely superfluous and could be deleted without affecting the stories in any noticeable way.

It therefore seems likely that John Lane's insistence on a change of title led to Clovis being promoted from only one among several *enfants terribles* in Munro's work (Reginald, Bertie van Tahn, and later Comus Bassington in the 1912 novel *The Unbearable Bassington*) to Munro's best-known character. Indeed, Clovis stories continued to appear even after *The Chronicles of Clovis*. The present volume reprints for the first time 'The Romance of Business' (originally published in the *Daily News and Leader* on 19 March 1914). This is not the same story as 'Clovis on the Alleged Romance of Business' (published after Munro's death in *The Square Egg and Other Sketches*, date of composition unknown), though the similarity in title and theme suggests that the two were written around the same time. 'The Romance of Business' is unique among Munro's short stories in having been written to order. It appeared within a special full-page advertisement for the department store Selfridge's. Munro's text only takes up a small proportion of the page, two thirds of which are filled by an elaborate illustration of laden men, trucks and even elephants passing through an ornate classical archway on their way to a dock with cargo ships. Selfridge's commissioned several such illustrations from noted artists, complemented by short texts on subjects such as "The Dignity of Work", "Imagination" and "Markets of the World", and had them printed in a number of prominent newspapers as part of its fifth birthday celebrations. One can assume that Munro was assigned the phrase "the romance of business". 'Clovis on the Alleged Romance of Business' may even have been a first attempt that was (unsurprisingly) rejected by Selfridge's: it consists of a monologue by Clovis in which he emphatically rejects the idea and mocks businessmen for their methodical dullness.

In the *Daily News and Leader* text we can see Munro riffing on a number of familiar elements. The story features Clovis and an aunt (though not the same aunt as in 'The Secret Sin of Septimus Brope', whose surname is Troyle, not Sangrail; presumably he has several, like Bertie Wooster). The plot involves a trick played upon an objectionable third party, which is a common 'Saki' plot type. In this case, Clovis is a listener, just as he is in the tale of 'Esmé', but he does get the final word, affirming that his aunt's actions have "brought the Romance of Business to an advanced stage of perfection". Whoever handled Selfridge's advertising account seems not to have noticed Clovis's (or Munro's) sly insinuation that the charm of business consists of misrepresenting facts and manipulating demand for one's own financial gain. The story is at any rate at odds with the rather earnest tributes in the other advertisements (and probably the better for it).

The second 'new' story printed here is 'Mrs. Pendercoet's Lost Identity', which has lain forgotten for over a hundred years between the pages of *The Odd Volume* for 1911. *The Odd Volume* was an illustrated anthology published yearly between 1908 and 1917 to raise funds for the National Book Trade Provident Society, a charity set up in the previous century to provide for "decaying [sic] booksellers and their spouses" (Wilson 2022). The main characters in this story are the aforementioned Mrs. Pendercoet and a youth of eighteen given to flippant comments and practical jokes. The story itself is reminiscent of those involving Reginald and the Duchess, or Clovis and one of Munro's self-important females such as the Baroness, Mrs. Packletide or Lady Bastable. Indeed, if it had been destined for *The Chronicles of Clovis*, it may even have featured Clovis, but it was not, and so Mrs. Pendercoet's young foil is called not Clovis but Rollo.

Finally, this volume also reprints 'The Optimist', which has unaccountably been omitted from collections until now. It is a fine example of another facet of 'Saki'. Although the scenario's starting point is similar to that of 'Esmé', with the protagonist getting separated from the pack while out hunting, 'The Optimist' shows Munro writing in a more naturalistic vein, slowly building an atmosphere of unease before springing a surprise ending on both the main character and the reader.

Returning to the subject of changes Munro made for *The Chronicles of Clovis*, one story remains to be discussed, for it represents a special case. In a letter dated 19 June 1911, Munro rejects John Lane's suggestion that he write something "of an immediately topical nature, such as a story dealing with the Coronation [of George V on 22 June 1911], as it gives the book an air of out-of-dateness almost as soon as it [is] published" (Gibson 225, letter #6). In the end, he capitulated to his publisher on this, writing 'The Recessional', which basically recycles the main idea of 'Reginald's Peace Poem' (1902) but with Clovis instead of Reginald and the coronation instead of the end of the Boer War. Nevertheless, Munro's expressed reluctance here makes his silent acquiescence to the inclusion of the story 'Ministers of Grace' in *The Chronicles of Clovis* more surprising. Although published in 1910 in the *Bystander* magazine, it was not one of the stories Munro had suggested for inclusion in a book collection when he first approached John Lane. 'Ministers of Grace' is a piece of political satire which can only be understood properly if one knows something about the public figures being lampooned. The longer book version only compounded this problem by giving them false names, such as Quinston for Winston Churchill and Halfan Halfour for Arthur Balfour. It is unlikely this was done out of fear of complaints from those mocked in the story, as it was already clear from the periodical version who was meant. (The *Bystander* version even had illustrations.) Although the aliases Munro chose are far from being impenetrable, he still seems to have felt the reader might need some extra cues, such as when he glosses "Cocksley Coxon" (the liberal theologian Canon Herbert Hensley Henson) as "one of the pillars of unorthodoxy in the Anglican Church" (Saki 2000: 221). This is just one example of a sort of ambivalence or half-heartedness in Munro's changes to this story. It might have been more logical to have cut the topical references entirely and given the story a more universal application, but apart from one timeless joke about the London public being less concerned about a *coup d'état* in Scotland than about the cricket being postponed, Munro did the opposite. In his new version, he widened the scope of his satire, including references to the Conservative MP Hugh Cecil and political hostesses and adding a section about the recent attacks on George Cadbury (a Quaker and supporter of the Liberals) by the *Evening News*, *Spectator* and other right-leaning publications. In rewriting, Munro nearly doubled the length of the story: it is the longest by far in *The Chronicles of Clovis* (just over 3600 words, as against its nearest rivals 'The Secret Sin of Septimus Brope' and 'The Story of St. Vespaluus', both of which come in at just under 3000 words each). Surprisingly, less than half of this increase is due to the added story elements mentioned above. The rest can justifiably be described as padding. This is principally achieved through additional incidental details ("The two men disappeared in the direction of the bun stall, *chatting volubly as they went*" [my emphasis]) and paraphrases of the sort whereby "probably" becomes "in all probability". Such prolixity was unusual for Munro; many of his most anthologised stories are a third of the length of this one. The correspondence suggests that John Lane was pressing Munro to reach a specific page target: in several letters Munro refers to "long" or "longish" stories (Gibson 224–26, letters #4, #5, #6, #7, #10) and one ends "Please let me know if you think you have now enough material" (Gibson 225, letter #6). Modern readers—who now have the chance to compare the two versions—may be reminded of the saying that "brevity is the soul of wit".

Taken as a whole, the history of these stories illuminates the interaction of freelance author, newspaper editor, book publisher and reading public. Munro's principal interest in his stories was to make money from them as quickly and easily as possible. He changed publisher in the hope of better sales and agreed to alter his works to make them fit a format that his new publisher deemed easier to sell, but he apparently was not motivated to put much effort into tailoring his stories to meet these demands. Instead, his revisions were cursory, aimed at satisfying John Lane (in terms of length) and "non-literary" readers who (publishers believed) wanted some predictability in a book of short stories.

The main motive behind this publication is to allow readers to read these stories without their later distortions and thereby gain an idea of the skill, imagination and versatility that made Munro successful in the first place. It makes available the stories as originally composed, as well as the three forgotten tales already mentioned. The parts of the texts that Munro changed are printed in grey, which makes them discernible but not distracting for the reader. The variants can then be found at the end of the book. In the electronic version they are linked so that the reader can easily jump from story to variants and back again. I have also included information on the place and date of first publication, and provided notes to explain references and allusions that may not be readily understandable to a twenty-first-century public. In so doing, I hope to give readers the opportunity to enjoy the stories as their first readers could.

References

Baldwin, Dean R. 2013. *Art and Commerce in the British Short Story, 1880–1950* (London: Pickering & Chatto), https://doi.org/10.4324/9781315655390

'Books and Booksellers'. 1911, Wednesday 8 November. *London Daily News*, p. 4.

Frost, Adam. 2001. 'The Letters of H. H. Munro: Unfinished Business', *English Literature in Transition, 1880–1920*, 44.2, 199–204.

Gaston, Bruce. [n.d.] *First publication*, https://www.annotated-saki.info/first-publication

Gibson, Brian. 2014. *Reading Saki: The Fiction of H. H. Munro* (Jefferson, NC: McFarland).

Lewis, Karen L. 2004. 'The Victorian Short Story: A Textual Culture's Forgotten Genre' (unpublished doctoral dissertation, Rice University), https://hdl.handle.net/1911/18661

Milne, A. A. 1926. 'Introduction', in *The Chronicles of Clovis* (London: John Lane The Bodley Head), pp. ix–xiii.

Saki (H. H. Munro). 2000. *Saki. The Complete Short Stories*, new ed. (Harmondsworth: Penguin Classics).

—. 1911. 'Mrs. Pendercoet's Lost Identity', in *The Odd Volume*, ed. by John G. Wilson (London: Simpkin, Marshall, Hamilton), pp. 20–21.

Wilson, Colin. 2022. 'Kings Langley. Dickinson House and The Retreat', *Herts Memories*, https://www.hertsmemories.org.uk/content/herts-history/towns-and-villages/kings-langley/kings-langley-dickinson-house-and-the-retreat

Zacks, Aaron Shanohn. 2012. 'Publishing Short Stories: British Modernist Fiction and the Literary Marketplace' (unpublished doctoral dissertation, University of Texas at Austin), http://hdl.handle.net/2152/ETD-UT-2012-08-6327

Chronology

18 Dec. 1870
Hector Hugh Munro is born in Akyab, Burma, third child of Mary Frances Mercer and Charles Augustus Munro, inspector-general of police.

1872
Mother dies in a freak accident; Munro and his brother and sister sent to live with their grandmother and aunts in England.

1882
Munro sent to board at Pencarwick School, Exmouth.

1885
Starts Bedford Grammar School.

1887–93
Munro's father retires and returns permanently from Burma; takes family on extended trips through Europe.

1893
Munro goes to Burma to work in the colonial police force.

1894
Returns to London on grounds of ill health.

1899
First publications: 'The Achievement of the Cat', anonymously in *Westminster Gazette*; 'Dogged', Munro's first published short story, in *St. Paul's Magazine*, credited to "H.H.M.".

1900
Publication of *The Rise of the Russian Empire* (London: Grant Richards), the fruit of several years' research in the British Library.
Munro's first political sketches are published in the *Westminister Gazette*.

1902
The Political Jungle Book and *Not So Stories* (political sketches) are published in the *Westminster Gazette*.
Publication of *The Westminster Alice*: political sketches with illustrations by F. Carruthers Gould (London: Westminster Gazette Office).

1902–08
Employed as foreign correspondent by the *Morning Post* in the Balkans, Warsaw, Russia, and Paris.

1904
Publication of *Reginald* (London: Methuen).

1908
Returns to London.

1910
Publication of *Reginald in Russia* (London: Methuen).

1911
Publication of *The Chronicles of Clovis* (London: John Lane, The Bodley Head).

1912
Publication of the novel *The Unbearable Bassington* (London: John Lane, The Bodley Head).

1913
Publication of the novel *When William Came: A Story of London Under the Hohenzollerns* (London: John Lane, The Bodley Head).

1914
Publication of *Beasts and Super-Beasts* (London: John Lane, The Bodley Head).
Death of father.

25 Aug. 1914
Enlists as a trooper in 2nd King Edward's Horse.

Sept. 1914
Transfers to 22nd Battalion, Royal Fusiliers.

Nov. 1915
Battalion is sent to France.

16 Nov. 1916
Shot and killed by a German sniper near Beaumont Hamel in northern France.

1919
Posthumous publication of *The Toys of Peace and Other Papers* (London: John Lane, The Bodley Head).

1924
Posthumous publication of *The Square Egg and Other Sketches* (London: John Lane, The Bodley Head).

1924
Publication of *The Watched Pot*, a play written in 1914 with Charles Maude (London: John Lane, The Bodley Head).

1926–27
Publication of *The Works of Saki* (London: John Lane, The Bodley Head, 8 volumes).

1930
Publication of *The Short Stories of Saki* (London: John Lane, The Bodley Head).
First performance of *The Watched Pot*.

1943
London première of *The Watched Pot*.

'Saki', photographed in 1913. https://en.wikipedia.org/wiki/File:Hector_Hugh_Munro_aka_Saki,_by_E_O_Hoppe,_1913.jpg#/media/File:Hector_Hugh_Munro_aka_Saki,_by_E_O_Hoppe,_1913.jpg

Esmé

Westminster Gazette, 17 December 1910, p. 3

"All hunting stories are the same," said the Irrelevant Man; "just as all Turf stories are the same, and all—"

"My hunting story isn't a bit like any you've ever heard," said the Baroness. "It happened quite a while ago, when I was about twenty-three. I wasn't living apart from my husband then; you see, neither of us could afford to make the other a separate allowance. In spite of everything that proverbs may say, poverty keeps together more homes than it breaks up. But we always hunted with different packs. All this has nothing to do with the story."

"We haven't arrived at the meet yet. I suppose there was a meet," said the Irrelevant Man.

"Of course there was a meet," said the Baroness; "all the usual crowd were there, especially Constance Broddle. Constance is one of those strapping florid girls that go so well with autumn scenery or Christmas decorations in church. 'I feel a presentiment that something dreadful is going to happen,' she said to me; 'am I looking pale?'

"She was looking about as pale as a beetroot that has suddenly heard bad news.

"'You're looking nicer than usual,' I said, 'but that's so easy for you.' Before she had got the right bearings of this remark we had settled down to business; hounds had found a fox lying out in some gorse-bushes."

"I knew it," said the Man, "in every fox-hunting story that I've ever heard there's been a fox and some gorse-bushes."

"Constance and I were well mounted," continued the Baroness serenely, "and we had no difficulty in keeping ourselves in the first flight, though it was a fairly stiff run. Towards the finish, however, we must have held rather too independent a line, for we lost the hounds, and found ourselves plodding aimlessly along miles away from anywhere. It was fairly exasperating, and my temper was beginning to let itself go by inches, when on pushing our way through an accommodating hedge we were gladdened by the sight of hounds in full cry in a hollow just beneath us.

"'There they go,' cried Constance, and then added in a gasp, 'In Heaven's name, what are they hunting?'

"It was certainly no mortal fox. It stood more than twice as high, had a short, ugly head, and an enormous thick neck.

"'It's a hyæna,' I cried; 'it must have escaped from Lord Pabham's Park.'

"At that moment the hunted beast turned and faced its pursuers, and the hounds (there were only about six couple of them) stood round in a half-circle and looked foolish. Evidently they had broken away from the rest of the pack on the trail of this alien scent, and were not quite sure how to treat their quarry now they had got him.

"The hyæna hailed our approach with unmistakable relief and demonstrations of friendliness. It had probably been accustomed to uniform kindness from humans, while its first experience of a pack of hounds had left a bad impression. The hounds looked more than ever embarrassed as their quarry paraded its sudden intimacy with us, and the faint toot of a horn in the distance was seized on as a welcome signal for unobtrusive departure. Constance and I and the hyæna were left alone in the gathering twilight.

"'What are we to do?' asked Constance.

"'What a person you are for questions,' I said.

"'Well, we can't stay here all night with a hyæna,' she retorted.

"'I don't know what your ideas of comfort are,' I said; 'but I shouldn't think of staying here all night even without a hyæna. My home may be an unhappy one, but at least it has hot and cold water laid on, and domestic service, and other conveniences which we shouldn't find here. We had better make for that ridge of trees to the right; I imagine the Crowley road is just beyond.'[1]

"We trotted off slowly along a faintly marked cart-track, with the beast following cheerfully at our heels.

---

1   Possibly invented, though there is a township called Crowley in Cheshire.

"'What on earth are we to do with the hyæna?' came the inevitable question.

"'What does one generally do with hyænas?' I asked crossly.

"'I've never had anything to do with one before,' said Constance.

"'Well, neither have I. If we even knew its sex we might give it a name. Perhaps we might call it Esmé.² That would do in either case.'

"There was still sufficient daylight for us to distinguish wayside objects, and our listless spirits gave an upward perk as we came upon a small half-naked gipsy brat picking blackberries from a low-growing bush. The sudden apparition of two horsewomen and a hyæna set it off crying, and in any case we should scarcely have gleaned any useful geographical information from that source; but there was a probability that we might strike a gipsy encampment somewhere along our route. We rode on hopefully but uneventfully for another mile or so.

"'I wonder what that child was doing there,' said Constance presently.

"'Picking blackberries. Obviously.'

"'I don't like the way it cried,' pursued Constance; 'somehow its wail keeps ringing in my ears.'

"I did not chide Constance for her morbid fancies; as a matter of fact the same sensation, of being pursued by a persistent, fretful wail, had been forcing itself on my rather over-tired nerves. For company's sake I hulloed to Esmé, who had lagged somewhat behind. With a few springy bounds he drew up level, and then shot past us.

"The wailing accompaniment was explained. The gipsy child was firmly, and I expect painfully, held in his jaws.

"'Merciful Heaven!' screamed Constance, 'what on earth shall we do? What are we to do?'

"I am perfectly certain that at the Last Judgment Constance will ask more questions than any of the examining Seraphs.

"'Can't we do something?' she persisted tearfully, as Esmé cantered easily along in front of our tired horses.

"Personally I was doing everything that occurred to me at the moment. I stormed and scolded and coaxed in English and French and gamekeeper language; I made absurd, ineffectual cuts in the air with

---

2   The name, whose origins are old French, was originally a male one but came to be given to girls as well. Its meaning — singularly unsuitable here — is "loved".

my thongless hunting-crop; I hurled my sandwich case at the brute; in fact, I really don't know what more I could have done. And still we lumbered on through the deepening dusk, with that dark, uncouth shape lumbering ahead of us, and a drone of lugubrious music floating in our ears. Suddenly Esmé bounded aside into some thick bushes, where we could not follow; the wail rose to a shriek and then stopped altogether. This part of the story I always hurry over, because it is really rather horrible. When the beast joined us again, after an absence of a few minutes, there was an air of patient understanding about him, as though he knew that he had done something of which we disapproved, but which he felt to be thoroughly justifiable.

"'How can you let that ravening beast trot by your side?' asked Constance. She was looking more than ever like an albino beetroot.

"'In the first place, I can't prevent it,' I said; 'and in the second place, whatever else he may be, I doubt if he's ravening at the present moment.'

"Constance shuddered. 'Do you think the poor little thing suffered much?' came another of her futile questions.

"'The indications were all that way,' I said; 'on the other hand, of course, it may have been crying from sheer temper. Children sometimes do.'

"It was nearly pitch-dark when we emerged suddenly into the highroad. A flash of lights and the whir of a motor went past us at the same moment at uncomfortably close quarters. A thud and a sharp screeching yell followed a second later. The car drew up, and when I had ridden back to the spot I found a young man bending over a dark, motionless mass lying by the roadside.

"'You have killed my Esmé,' I exclaimed bitterly.

"'I'm so awfully sorry,' said the young man; 'I keep dogs myself, so I know what you must feel about it. I'll do anything I can in reparation.'

"'Please bury him at once,' I said; 'that much I think I may ask of you.'

"'Bring the spade, William,' he called to the chauffeur. Evidently hasty roadside interments were contingencies that had been provided against.

"The digging of a sufficiently large grave took some little time. 'I say, what a magnificent fellow,' said the motorist as the corpse was rolled over into the trench. 'I'm afraid he must have been rather a valuable animal.'

"'He took second in the puppy class at Birmingham last year,' I said resolutely.[3]

"Constance snorted loudly.

"'Don't cry, dear,' I said brokenly; 'it was all over in a moment. He couldn't have suffered much.'

"'Look here,' said the young fellow desperately, 'you simply must let me do something by way of reparation.'

"I refused sweetly, but as he persisted I let him have my address.

"Of course, we kept our own counsel as to the earlier episodes of the evening. Lord Pabham never advertised the loss of his hyæna; when a strictly fruit-eating animal strayed from his park a year or two previously he was called upon to give compensation in eleven cases of sheep-worrying and to practically re-stock his neighbours' poultry-yards, and an escaped hyæna would have mounted up to something on the scale of a Government[4] grant. The gipsies were equally unobtrusive over their missing offspring; I don't suppose in large encampments they really know to a child or two how many they've got."

The Baroness paused reflectively, and then continued:

"There was a sequel to the adventure, though. I got through the post a charming little diamond brooch, with the name Esmé set in a sprig of rosemary. Incidentally, too, I lost the friendship of Constance Broddle. You see, when I sold the brooch I quite properly refused to give her any share of the proceeds. I pointed out that the Esmé part of the affair was my own invention, and the hyæna-part of it belonged to Lord Pabham, if it really was his hyæna, of which, of course, I've no proof."

---

3   The National Dog Show has been organised by the Birmingham Dog Show Society since 1859.
4   Capitalised in the original.

Tobermory

Westminster Gazette, 27 November 1909, p. 2

It was a chill, rain-washed afternoon of a late August day, that indefinite season when partridges are still in security or cold storage, and there is nothing to hunt—unless one is bounded on the north by the Bristol Channel, in which case one may lawfully gallop after fat red stags.[1] Lady Blemley's house-party was not bounded on the north by the Bristol Channel, hence there was a full gathering of her guests round the tea-table on this particular afternoon. And, in spite of the blankness of the season and the triteness of the occasion, there was no trace in the company of that fatigued restlessness which means a dread of the pianola and a subdued hankering for auction bridge. The undisguised open-mouthed attention of the entire party was fixed on the homely negative personality of Mr. Cornelius Appin. Of all her guests, he was the one who had come to Lady Blemley with the vaguest reputation. Someone had said he was "clever," and he had got his invitation in the moderate expectation, on the part of his hostess, that some portion at least of his cleverness would be contributed to the general entertainment. Until tea-time that day she had been unable to discover in what direction, if any, his cleverness lay. He was neither a wit nor a croquet champion, a hypnotic force nor a begetter of amateur theatricals. Neither did his exterior suggest the sort of man in whom women are willing to pardon a generous measure of mental deficiency. He had subsided into mere Mr. Appin, and the Cornelius seemed a piece of transparent baptismal bluff. And now he was claiming to have launched on the world a discovery beside which the invention of gunpowder, of the printing-press, and

---

1   The partridge hunting season begins in the UK on 1 September; hunting with staghounds (a practice limited to Devon and Somerset) was allowed from August.

of steam locomotion were inconsiderable trifles. Science had made bewildering strides in many directions during recent decades, but this thing seemed to belong to the domain of miracle rather than to scientific achievement.

"And do you really ask us to believe," Sir Wilfrid was saying, "that you have discovered a means for instructing animals in the art of human speech, and that dear old Tobermory has proved your first successful pupil?"

"It is a problem at which I have worked for the last seventeen years," said Mr. Appin, "but only during the last eight or nine months have I been rewarded with glimmerings of success. Of course I have experimented with thousands of animals, but latterly only with cats, those wonderful creatures which have assimilated themselves so marvellously with our civilization while retaining all their highly developed feral instincts. Here and there among cats one comes across an outstanding superior intellect, just as one does among the ruck of human beings, and when I made the acquaintance of Tobermory a week ago I saw at once that I was in contact with a 'Beyond-cat' of extraordinary intelligence. I had gone far along the road to success in recent experiments; with Tobermory, as you call him, I have reached the goal."

Mr. Appin concluded his remarkable statement in a voice which he strove to divest of a triumphant inflection. No one said "rats," though Bertie van Tahn's lips moved in a monosyllabic contortion which probably invoked those rodents of disbelief.

"And do you mean to say," asked Miss Resker, after a slight pause, "that you have taught Tobermory to say and understand easy sentences of one syllable?"

"My dear Miss Resker," said the wonder-worker patiently, "one teaches little children and savages and backward adults in that piecemeal fashion; when one has once solved the problem of making a beginning with an animal of highly developed intelligence one has no need for those halting methods. Tobermory can speak our language with perfect correctness."

This time Bertie van Tahn very distinctly said, "Beyond-rats!" Sir Wilfrid was more polite, but equally sceptical.

"Hadn't we better have the cat in and judge for ourselves?" suggested Lady Blemley.

Sir Wilfrid went in search of the animal, and the company settled themselves down to the languid expectation of witnessing some more or less adroit drawing-room ventriloquism.

In a minute Sir Wilfrid was back in the room, his face white beneath its tan and his eyes dilated with excitement.

"By Gad, it's true!"

His agitation was unmistakably genuine, and his hearers started forward in a thrill of awakened interest.

Collapsing into an armchair, he continued breathlessly: "I found him dozing in the smoking-room, and called out to him to come for his tea. He blinked at me in his usual way, and I said, 'Come on, Toby; don't keep us waiting'; and, by Gad! he drawled out in a most horribly natural voice that he'd come when he dashed well pleased! I nearly jumped out of my skin!"

Appin had preached to absolutely incredulous hearers; Sir Wilfrid's statement carried instant conviction. A Babel-like chorus of startled exclamation arose, amid which the scientist sat mutely enjoying the first fruit of his stupendous discovery.

In the midst of the clamour Tobermory entered the room and made his way with velvet tread and studied unconcern across to the group seated round the tea-table.

A sudden hush of awkwardness and constraint fell on the company. Somehow there seemed an element of embarrassment in addressing on equal terms a domestic cat of acknowledged mental ability.

"Will you have some milk, Tobermory?" asked Lady Blemley in a rather strained voice.

"I don't mind if I do," was the response, couched in a tone of even indifference. A shiver of suppressed excitement went through the listeners, and Lady Blemley might be excused for pouring out the saucerful of milk rather unsteadily.

"I'm afraid I've spilt a good deal of it," she said apologetically.

"After all, it's not my Axminster," was Tobermory's rejoinder.

Another silence fell on the group, and then Miss Resker, in her best district-visitor manner, asked if the human language had been difficult to learn. Tobermory looked squarely at her for a moment and then fixed his gaze serenely on the middle distance. It was obvious that boring questions lay outside his scheme of life.

"What do you think of human intelligence?" asked Mavis Pellington lamely.

"Of whose intelligence in particular?" asked Tobermory coldly.

"Oh, well, mine for instance," said Mavis, with a feeble laugh.

"You put me in an embarrassing position," said Tobermory, whose tone and attitude certainly did not suggest a shred of embarrassment. "When your inclusion in this house-party was suggested Sir Wilfrid protested that you were the most brainless woman of his acquaintance, and that there was a wide distinction between hospitality and the care of the feeble-minded. Lady Blemley replied that your lack of brain-power was the precise quality which had earned you your invitation, as you were the only person she could think of who might be idiotic enough to buy their old car. You know, the one they call 'The Envy of Sisyphus,' because it goes quite nicely up hill[2] if you push it."[3]

Lady Blemley's protestations would have had greater effect if she had not casually suggested to Mavis only that morning that the car in question would be just the thing for her down at her Devonshire home.

Major Barfield plunged in heavily to effect a diversion.

"How about your carryings-on with the tortoiseshell puss up at the stables, eh?"

The moment he had said it everyone realised the blunder.

"One does not usually discuss these matters in public," said Tobermory frigidly. "From a slight observation of your ways since you've been in this house I should imagine you'd find it inconvenient if I were to shift the conversation on to your own little affairs."

The panic which ensued was not confined to the Major.

"Would you like to go and see if cook has got your dinner ready?" suggested Lady Blemley hurriedly, affecting to ignore the fact that it wanted at least two hours to Tobermory's dinner-time.

"Thanks," said Tobermory, "not quite so soon after my tea. I don't want to die of indigestion."

"Cats have nine lives, you know," said Sir Wilfrid heartily.

"Possibly," answered Tobermory; "but only one liver."

"Adelaide!" said Mrs. Cornett, "do you mean to encourage that cat to

---

2   Two words in the original.
3   In Greek mythology, Sisyphus was condemned to spend eternity pushing a boulder uphill, only to have it roll back down each time.

go out and gossip about us in the servants' hall?"

The panic had indeed become general. A narrow ornamental balustrade ran in front of most of the bedroom windows at the Towers, and it was recalled with dismay that this had formed a favourite promenade for Tobermory at all hours, whence he could watch the pigeons—and heaven knew what else besides. If he intended to become reminiscent in his present outspoken strain the effect would be something more than disconcerting. Mrs. Cornett, who spent much time at her toilet table, and whose complexion was reputed to be of a nomadic though punctual disposition, looked as ill at ease as the Major. Miss Scrawen, who wrote fiercely sensuous poetry and led a blameless life, merely displayed irritation; if you are methodical and virtuous in private you don't necessarily want everyone to know it. Bertie van Tahn, who was so depraved at seventeen that he had long ago given up trying to be any worse, turned a dull shade of gardenia white, but he did not commit the error of dashing out of the room like Odo Finsberry, a young gentleman who was understood to be reading for the Church and who was possibly disturbed at the thought of scandals he might hear concerning other people.

Even in a delicate situation like the present, Agnes Resker could not endure to remain too long in the background.

"Why did I ever come down here?" she asked dramatically.

Tobermory immediately accepted the opening.

"Judging by what you said to Mrs. Cornett on the croquet-lawn yesterday, you were out for food. You described the Blemleys as the dullest people to stay with that you knew, but said they were clever enough to employ a first-rate cook; otherwise they'd find it difficult to get anyone to come down a second time."

"There's not a word of truth in it! I appeal to Mrs. Cornett—" exclaimed the discomfited Agnes.

"Mrs. Cornett repeated your remark afterwards to Bertie van Tahn," continued Tobermory, "and said, 'That woman is a regular Hunger Marcher;[4] she'd go anywhere for four square meals a day,' and Bertie van Tahn said—"

---

4 Hunger marches were a form of social protest by the unemployed to draw attention to their lack of money to buy food; at the time the term was quite new.

At this point the chronicle mercifully ceased. Tobermory had caught a glimpse of the big yellow Tom from the Rectory working his way through the shrubbery towards the stable wing. In a flash he had vanished through the open French window.

With the disappearance of his too brilliant pupil Cornelius Appin found himself beset by a hurricane of bitter upbraiding, anxious inquiry, and frightened entreaty. The responsibility for the situation lay with him, and he must prevent matters from becoming worse. Could Tobermory impart his dangerous gift to other cats? was the first question he had to answer. It was possible, he replied, that he might have initiated his intimate friend the stable puss into his new accomplishment, but it was unlikely that his teaching could have taken a wider range as yet.

"Then," said Mrs. Cornett, "Tobermory may be a valuable cat and a great pet; but I'm sure you'll agree, Adelaide, that both he and the stable cat must be done away with without delay."

"You don't suppose I've enjoyed the last quarter of an hour, do you?" said Lady Blemley bitterly. "My husband and I are very fond of Tobermory—at least, we were before this horrible accomplishment was infused into him; but now, of course, the only thing is to have him destroyed as soon as possible."

"We can put some strychnine in the scraps he always gets at dinner-time," said Sir Wilfrid, "and I will go and drown the stable cat myself. The coachman will be very sore at losing his pet, but I'll say a very catching form of mange has broken out in both cats and we're afraid of it spreading to the kennels."

"But my great discovery!" expostulated Mr. Appin; "after all my years of research and experiment—"

"You can go and experiment on the shorthorns at the farm, who are under proper control," said Mrs. Cornett, "or the elephants at the Zoological Gardens. They're said to be highly intelligent, and they have this recommendation, that they don't come creeping about our bedrooms and under chairs, and so forth."

An archangel ecstatically proclaiming the Millennium, and then finding that it clashed unpardonably with Henley[5] and would have to be indefinitely postponed, could hardly have felt more crestfallen than

---

5   The regatta at Henley-on-Thames was a fixture in the social calendar.

Cornelius Appin at the reception of his wonderful achievement. Public opinion, however, was against him—in fact, had the general voice been consulted on the subject it is probable that a strong minority vote would have been in favour of including him in the strychnine diet.

Defective train arrangements and a nervous desire to see matters brought to a finish prevented an immediate dispersal of the party; but dinner that evening was not a social success. Sir Wilfrid had had rather a trying time with the stable cat and subsequently with the coachman. Agnes Resker ostentatiously limited her repast to a morsel of dry toast, which she bit as though it were a personal enemy; while Mavis Pellington maintained a vindictive silence throughout the meal. Lady Blemley kept up a flow of what she hoped was conversation, but her attention was fixed on the doorway. A plateful of carefully dosed fish scraps was in readiness on the sideboard, but sweets and savoury and dessert went their way, and no Tobermory appeared either in the dining-room or kitchen.

The sepulchral dinner was cheerful compared with the subsequent vigil in the smoking-room. Eating and drinking had at least supplied a distraction and cloak to the prevailing embarrassment. Bridge was out of the question in the general tension of nerves and tempers, and after Odo Finsberry had given a lugubrious rendering of "Melisande in the Wood"[6] to a frigid audience music was tacitly avoided. At eleven the servants went to bed, announcing that the small window in the pantry had been left open as usual for Tobermory's private use. The guests read steadily through the current batch of magazines, and fell back gradually on the "Badminton Library"[7] and bound volumes of "Punch."[8] Lady Blemley made periodic visits to the pantry, returning each time with an expression of listless depression which forestalled questioning.

At two o'clock Bertie van Tahn broke the dominating silence.

"He won't turn up to-night. He's probably in the local newspaper office at the present moment, dictating the first instalment of his

---

6 From the poetry collection *Song of Dreams* by Ethel Clifford (1876–1959), set to music by Alma Goetz (?–?), 1902.

7 In full, *The Badminton Library of Sports and Pastimes*, a series of books, each devoted to a particular sport or activity (though ironically badminton was not one of them).

8 Very popular humorous and satirical magazine, founded 1841.

reminiscences. What's-her-name's book won't be in it.⁹ It will be the event of the day."

Having made this contribution to the general cheerfulness, Bertie van Tahn went to bed. At long intervals the various members of the house-party followed his example.

The servants taking round the early tea made a uniform announcement in reply to a uniform question. Tobermory had not returned.

Breakfast was, if anything, a more unpleasant function than dinner had been, but before its conclusion the situation was relieved. Tobermory's corpse was brought in from the shrubbery, where a gardener had just discovered it. From the bites on his throat and the yellow fur which coated his claws it was evident that he had fallen in unequal combat with the big Tom from the Rectory.

By midday most of the guests had quitted the Towers, and after lunch Lady Blemley had sufficiently recovered her spirits to write an extremely nasty letter to the Rectory about the loss of her valuable pet.

Tobermory had been Appin's one successful pupil, and he was destined to have no successor. A few weeks later an elephant in the Dresden Zoological Garden, which had shown no previous signs of irritability, broke loose and killed an Englishman who had apparently been teasing it. The victim's name was variously reported in the papers as Oppin and Eppelin, but his front name was faithfully rendered Cornelius.

"If he was trying German irregular verbs on the poor beast," said Bertie van Tahn, "he deserved all he got."

---

9   Possibly *Memories of Fifty Years*, the memoirs of society hostess Lady St. Helier (1845–1931), published the month before this story first appeared in print, but more probably *My Recollections* by Lady Cardigan, Countess of Cardigan and Comtesse de Lancastre (1824–1915), who scandalised Victorian society in her youth with her behaviour and Edwardian society in her old age with her memoirs (published 1909).

Mrs. Packletide's Tiger

The Bystander, 12 April 1911, pp. 68, 70[1]

It was Mrs. Packletide's pleasure and intention that she should shoot a tiger. Not that the lust to kill had suddenly descended on her, or that she felt that she would leave India safer and more wholesome than she had found it, with one fraction less of wild beast per million of inhabitants. The compelling motive for her sudden deviation towards the footsteps of Nimrod[2] was the fact that Loona Bimberton had recently been carried eleven miles in an aeroplane by an Algerian aviator, and talked of nothing else; only a personally procured tiger-skin and a heavy harvest of press photographs could successfully counter that sort of thing. Mrs. Packletide had already arranged in her mind the lunch she would give at her house in Curzon Street,[3] ostensibly in Loona Bimberton's honour, with a tiger-skin rug occupying most of the foreground and all of the conversation. She had also already designed in her mind the tiger-claw brooch that she was going to give Loona Bimberton on her next birthday. In a world that is supposed to be chiefly swayed by hunger and by love Mrs. Packletide was an exception; her movements and motives were largely governed by dislike of Loona Bimberton.

Circumstances proved propitious. Mrs. Packletide had offered a thousand rupees for the opportunity of shooting a tiger without overmuch risk or exertion, and it so happened that a neighbouring village could boast of being the favoured rendezvous of an animal of respectable antecedents, which had been driven by the increasing infirmities of age to abandon game-killing and confine its appetite to the

---

1   *Sic*. Page 69 has an unrelated full-page cartoon.
2   Biblical hunter. See Genesis 10. 8–9 and I Chronicles 1. 10.
3   In Mayfair, London; populated by the aristocracy and upper-class.

smaller domestic animals. The prospect of earning the thousand rupees had stimulated the sporting and commercial instinct of the villagers; children were posted night and day on the outskirts of the local jungle to head the tiger back in the unlikely event of his attempting to roam away to fresh hunting-grounds, and the cheaper kinds of goats were left about with elaborate carelessness to keep him satisfied with his present quarters. The one great anxiety was lest he should die of old age before the date appointed for the memsahib's[4] shoot. Mothers carrying their babies home through the jungle after the day's work in the fields hushed their singing lest they might curtail the restful sleep of the venerable herd-robber.

The great night duly arrived, moonlit and cloudless. A platform had been constructed in a comfortable and conveniently placed tree, and thereon crouched Mrs. Packletide and her paid companion, Miss Mebbin. A goat, gifted with a particularly persistent bleat, such as even a partially deaf tiger might be reasonably expected to hear on a still night, was tethered at the correct distance. With an accurately sighted rifle and a thumb-nail pack of patience cards the sportswoman awaited the coming of the quarry.

"I suppose we are in some danger?" said Miss Mebbin.

She was not actually nervous about the wild beast, but she had a morbid dread of performing an atom more service than she had been paid for.

"Nonsense," said Mrs. Packletide; "it's a very old tiger. It couldn't spring up here even if it wanted to."

"If it's an old tiger I think you ought to get it cheaper. A thousand rupees is a lot of money."

Louisa Mebbin adopted a protective elder-sister attitude towards money in general, irrespective of nationality or denomination. Her energetic intervention had saved many a rouble from dissipating itself in tips in some Moscow hotel, and francs and centimes clung to her instinctively under circumstances which would have driven them headlong from less sympathetic hands. Her speculations as to the market depreciation of tiger remnants were cut short by the appearance on the scene of the animal itself. As soon as it caught sight of the tethered goat

---

4   Indian term of respect for a female European.

it lay flat on the earth, seemingly less from a desire to take advantage of all available cover than for the purpose of snatching a short rest before commencing the grand attack.

"I believe it's ill," said Louisa Mebbin, loudly in Hindustani, for the benefit of the village headman, who was in ambush in a neighbouring tree.

"Hush!" said Mrs. Packletide, and at that moment the tiger commenced ambling towards his victim.

"Now, now!" urged Miss Mebbin with some excitement; "if he doesn't touch the goat we needn't pay for it." (The bait was an extra.)

The rifle flashed out with a loud report, and the great tawny beast sprang to one side and then rolled over in the stillness of death. In a moment a crowd of excited natives had swarmed on to the scene, and their shouting speedily carried the glad news to the village, where a thumping of tom-toms took up the chorus of triumph. And their triumph and rejoicing found a ready echo in the heart of Mrs. Packletide; already that luncheon-party in Curzon Street seemed immeasurably nearer.

It was Louisa Mebbin who drew attention to the fact that the goat was in death-throes from a mortal bullet-wound, while no trace of the rifle's deadly work could be found on the tiger. Evidently the wrong animal had been hit, and the beast of prey had succumbed to heart-failure, caused by the sudden report of the rifle, accelerated by senile decay. Mrs. Packletide was pardonably annoyed at the discovery; but, at any rate, she was the possessor of a dead tiger, and the villagers, anxious for their thousand rupees, gladly connived at the fiction that she had shot the beast. And Miss Mebbin was a paid companion. Therefore did Mrs. Packletide face the cameras with a light heart, and her pictured fame reached from the pages of the *Texas Weekly Snapshot* to the illustrated Monday supplement of the *Novoe Vremya*.[5] As for Loona Bimberton, she refused to look at an illustrated paper for weeks, and her letter of thanks for the gift of a tiger-claw brooch was a model of repressed emotions. The luncheon-party she declined; there are limits beyond which repressed emotions become dangerous.

From Curzon Street the tiger-skin rug travelled down to the Manor House, and was duly inspected and admired by the county, and it

---

5   Russian newspaper published in St. Petersburg.

seemed a fitting and appropriate thing when Mrs. Packletide went to the County Costume Ball in the character of Diana.⁶

"How amused everyone would be if they knew what really happened," said Louisa Mebbin a few days after the ball.

"What do you mean?" asked Mrs. Packletide quickly.

"How you shot the goat and frightened the tiger to death," said Miss Mebbin with her disagreeably pleasant laugh.

"No one would believe it," said Mrs. Packletide, her face changing colour as rapidly as though it were going through a book of patterns⁷ before post-time.⁸

"Loona Bimberton would," said Miss Mebbin. Mrs. Packletide's face settled on an unbecoming shade of greenish white.

"You surely wouldn't give me away?" she asked.

"I've seen a week-end cottage near Dorking that I should rather like to buy," said Miss Mebbin with seeming irrelevance. "Six hundred and eighty, freehold. Quite a bargain, only I don't happen to have the money."

* * * * *

Louisa Mebbin's pretty week-end cottage, christened by her 'Les Fauves'⁹ and gay in summer-time with its garden borders of tiger-lilies, is the wonder and admiration of her friends.

"It is a marvel how Louisa manages to do it," is the general verdict.

Mrs. Packletide indulges in no more big-game shooting.

"The incidental expenses are so heavy," she confides to inquiring friends.

---

6 Roman goddess of the hunt.
7 Catalogue of the colours worn by racehorses and their jockeys.
8 The starting time for a horse race (and therefore the deadline for placing a bet).
9 'The wild animals' (French).

The Background

Leinsters' Magazine, July 1910 (No. 4, vol. 1), pp. 284–85[1]

Henri Deplis was by birth a native of the Grand Duchy of Luxemburg. On maturer reflection he became a commercial traveller. His business activities frequently took him beyond the limits of the Grand Duchy, and he was stopping in a small town of Northern Italy when news reached him from home that a legacy from a distant and deceased relative had fallen to his share.

It was not a large legacy, even from the modest standpoint of Henri Deplis, but it impelled him towards some seemingly harmless extravagances. In particular it led him to patronise local art as represented by the tattoo-needles of Signor Andreas Pincini. Signor Pincini was, perhaps, the most brilliant master of tattoo craft that Italy had ever known, but his circumstances were decidedly impoverished, and for the sum of six hundred francs he gladly undertook to cover his client's back, from the collar-bone down to the waistline, with a glowing representation of the Fall of Icarus.[2] The design, when finally developed,

---

1   Originally called *The Journal of the Leinster Regiment, Leinsters' Magazine* was the in-house newspaper of a regiment of the British Army, The Prince of Wales's Leinster Regiment (Royal Canadians). The magazine was founded around 1909 while the regiment was in Devonport and was a short-lived but noticeable success under its editor Captain R. F. Legge and sub-editor Captain R. M. Raynsford. Care was taken over its illustrations, layout and printing, and it favoured articles and other pieces (including light verse) that would appeal to a general audience rather than publishing information that would only interest members of the regiment. It was around this period that Munro started looking for other outlets for his work beyond his two regular customers, the *Westminster Gazette* and *Morning Post*. As well as 'The Background', *Leinsters' Magazine* published Munro's 'The Baker's Dozen' (October 1909, later collected in *Reginald in Russia*). It ceased publishing in 1911 when the regiment was transferred to India and Legge remained in the UK.

2   In Greek mythology, the inventor Daedalus made pairs of artificial wings for himself and his son Icarus so that they could fly out of the labyrinth in which they had been

was a slight disappointment to Monsieur Deplis, who had suspected Icarus of being a fortress taken by Wallenstein in the Thirty Years' War,[3] but he was more than satisfied with the execution of the work, which was acclaimed by all who had the privilege of seeing it as Pincini's masterpiece.

It was his greatest effort, and his last. Without even waiting to be paid, the illustrious craftsman departed this life, and was buried under an ornate tombstone, whose winged cherubs would have afforded singularly little scope for the exercise of his favourite art. There remained, however, the widow Pincini, to whom the six hundred francs were due. And thereupon arose the great crisis in the life of Henri Deplis, tarveller[4] of commerce. The legacy, under the stress of numerous little calls on its substance, had dwindled to very insignificant proportions, and when a pressing wine bill and sundry other current accounts had been paid, there remained little more than 430 francs to offer to the widow. The lady was properly indignant, not wholly, as she volubly explained, on account of the suggested writing-off of 170 francs, but also at the attempt to depreciate the value of her late husband's acknowledged masterpiece. In a week's time Deplis was obliged to reduce his offer to 405 francs, which circumstance fanned the widow's indignation into a fury. She cancelled the sale of the work of art, and a few days later Deplis learned with a sense of consternation that she had presented it to the municipality of Bergamo, which had gratefully accepted it. He left the neighbourhood as unobtrusively as possible, and was genuinely relieved when his business commands took him to Rome, where he hoped his identity and that of the famous picture might be lost sight of.

But he bore on his back the burden of the dead man's genius. On presenting himself one day in the steaming corridor of a vapour bath, he was at once hustled back into his clothes by the proprietor, who was a North Italian, and who emphatically refused to allow the celebrated Fall of Icarus to be publicly on view without the permission of the municipality of Bergamo. Public interest and official vigilance

---

       imprisoned. Ignoring his father's warnings, Icarus flew too close to the sun and the wax in his wings melted, whereupon he plunged to his death in the sea below.

3   Albrecht von Wallenstein (1583–1634), supreme commander of the armies of the Habsburg Monarchy and major figure in the Thirty Years' War (1618–1648).

4   Written thus in the original.

increased as the matter became more widely known, and Deplis was unable to take a simple dip in the sea or river on the hottest afternoon unless clothed up to the collarbone in a substantial bathing garment. Later on the authorities of Bergamo conceived the idea that salt water might be injurious to the masterpiece, and a perpetual injunction was obtained which debarred the muchly[5] harassed commercial traveller from sea bathing under any circumstances. Altogether, he was fervently thankful when his firm of employers found him a new range of activities in the neighbourhood of Bordeaux. His thankfulness, however, ceased abruptly at the Franco-Italian frontier. An imposing array of official force barred his departure, and he was sternly reminded of the stringent law which forbids the exportation of Italian works of art.

A diplomatic parley ensued between the Luxemburgian and Italian Governments, and at one time the European situation became overcast with the possibilities of trouble. But the Italian Government stood firm; it declined to concern itself in the least with the fortunes or even the existence of Henri Deplis, commercial traveller, but was immovable in its decision that the Fall of Icarus (by the late Pincini, Andreas) at present the property of the municipality of Bergamo, should not leave the country.

The excitement died down in time, but the unfortunate Deplis, who was of a constitutionally retiring disposition, found himself a few months later once more the storm-centre of a furious controversy. A certain German art expert, who had obtained from the municipality of Bergamo permission to inspect the famous masterpiece, declared it to be a spurious Pincini, probably the work of some pupil whom he had employed in his declining years. The evidence of Deplis on the subject was obviously worthless, as he had been under the influence of the customary narcotics during the long process of pricking in the design. The editor of an Italian art journal refuted the contentions of the German expert and undertook to prove that his private life did not conform to any modern standard of decency. The whole of Italy and Germany were drawn into the dispute, and the rest of Europe was soon involved in the quarrel. There were stormy scenes in the Spanish Parliament, and the University of Copenhagen bestowed a gold medal on the German expert

---

5   Written thus in the original.

(afterwards sending a commission to examine his proofs on the spot), while two Polish schoolboys in Paris committed suicide to show what *they* thought of the matter.

Meanwhile, the unhappy human background fared no better than before, and it was not surprising that he drifted into the ranks of Italian anarchists. Four times at least he was escorted to the frontier as a dangerous and undesirable foreigner, but he was always brought back as the Fall of Icarus (attributed to Pincini, Andreas, early Twentieth Century). And then one day, at an anarchist congress at Genoa, a fellow-worker, in the heat of debate, broke a phial full of corrosive liquid over his back. The red shirt that he was wearing mitigated the effects, but the Icarus was ruined beyond recognition. His assailant was severely reprimanded for assaulting a fellow-anarchist and received seven years' imprisonment for defacing a national art treasure. As soon as he was able to leave the hospital Henri Deplis was put across the frontier as an undesirable alien.

In the quieter streets of Paris, especially in the neighbourhood of the Ministry of Fine Arts, you may sometimes meet a depressed, anxious-looking man, who, if you pass him the time of day, will answer you with a slight Luxemburgian accent. He nurses the illusion that he is one of the lost arms of the Venus de Milo, and hopes that the French Government may be persuaded to buy him. On all other subjects I believe he is tolerably sane.

The Jesting of Arlington Stringham

Westminster Gazette, 20 August 1910, p. 2

Arlington Stringham made a joke in the House of Commons. It was a thin House, and a very thin joke; something about the Anglo-Saxon race having a great many angles. It is possible that it was unintentional, but a fellow-member, who did not wish it to be supposed that he was asleep because his eyes were shut, laughed. One or two of the papers noted "a laugh" in brackets, and another, which was notorious for the carelessness of its political news, mentioned "laughter." Things often begin in that way.

"Arlington made a joke in the House last night," said Eleanor Stringham to her mother; "in all the years we've been married neither of us has made jokes, and I don't like it now. I'm afraid it's the beginning of the rift in the lute."

"What lute?" said her mother.

"It's a quotation," said Eleanor.[1]

To say that anything was a quotation was an excellent method, in Eleanor's eyes, for withdrawing it from discussion, just as you could always defend indifferent lamb late in the season by saying "it's mutton."

And, of course, Arlington Stringham continued to tread the thorny path of conscious humour into which Fate had beckoned him.

"The country's looking very green, but, after all, that's what it's there for," he remarked to his wife two days later.

"That's very modern, and I dare say very clever, but I'm afraid it's

---

1 The reference is to Alfred, Lord Tennyson's *Idylls of the King*: "'Tis the little rift within the lute,/That by and by will make the music mute,/And, ever widening, slowly silence all."

wasted on me," she observed coldly. If she had known how much effort it had cost him to make the remark she might have greeted it in a kinder spirit. It is the tragedy of human endeavour that it works so often unseen and unguessed.

Arlington said nothing, not from injured pride, but because he was thinking hard for something to say. Eleanor mistook his silence for an assumption of tolerant superiority, and her anger prompted her to a further gibe.

"You had better tell it to Lady Isobel. I've no doubt she would appreciate it."

Lady Isobel was seen everywhere with a fawn-coloured collie at a time when everyone else kept nothing but Pekinese, and she had once eaten four green apples at an afternoon tea in the Botanical Gardens, so she was widely credited with a rather unpleasant wit. The censorious said she slept in a hammock and understood Yeats's poems,[2] but her family denied both stories.

"The rift is widening to an abyss," said Eleanor to her mother that afternoon.

"I should not tell that to anyone," remarked her mother, after long reflection.

"Naturally, I should not talk about it very much," said Eleanor, "but why shouldn't I mention it to anyone?"

"Because you can't have an abyss in a lute. There isn't room."

Eleanor's outlook on life did not improve as the afternoon wore on. The page-boy had brought from the library "By Mere And Wold" instead of "By Mere Chance,"[3] the book which everyone denied having read. The unwelcome substitute appeared to be a collection of nature notes contributed by the author to the pages of some Northern weekly, and when one had been prepared to plunge with disapproving mind into a regrettable chronicle of ill-spent lives it was intensely irritating to read "the dainty yellow-hammers are now with us and flaunt their jaundiced livery from every bush and hillock." Besides, the thing was so obviously untrue; either there must be hardly any bushes or hillocks in those parts or the country must be fearfully overstocked with yellow-hammers. The

---

2 William Butler Yeats, Irish writer (1865–1939). The poems he had published to date had been influenced by his interest in mythology and mysticism.

3 Both inventions.

thing scarcely seemed worth telling such a lie about. And the page-boy stood there, with his sleekly brushed and parted hair, and his air of chaste and callous indifference to the desires and passions of the world. Eleanor hated boys, and she would have liked to have whipped this one long and often. It was perhaps the yearning of a woman who had no children of her own.

She turned at random to another paragraph. "Lie quietly concealed in the fern and bramble in the gap by the old rowan tree, and you may see, almost every evening during early summer, a pair of lesser whitethroats creeping up and down the nettles and hedge-growth that mask their nesting-place."

The insufferable monotony of the proposed recreation! Eleanor would not have watched the most brilliant performance at His Majesty's Theatre for a single evening under such uncomfortable circumstances, and to be asked to watch lesser whitethroats creeping up and down a nettle "almost every evening" during the height of the season struck her as an imputation on her intelligence that was positively offensive. Impatiently she transferred her attention to the dinner menu, which the boy had thoughtfully brought in as an alternative to the more solid literary fare. "Rabbit curry" met her eye, and the lines of disapproval deepened on her already puckered brow. The cook was a great believer in the influence of environment, and nourished an obstinate conviction that if you brought rabbit and curry-powder together in one dish a rabbit curry would be the result. And the odious Bertie van Tahn was coming to dinner. Surely, thought Eleanor, if Arlington knew how much she had had that day to try her, he would refrain from joke-making.

It was Eleanor herself who mentioned the name of a certain statesman, who may be decently covered under the disguise of X.

"X.," said Arlington Stringham, "has the soul of a meringue."

It was a useful remark to have on hand, because it applied equally well to four prominent statesmen of the day, which quadrupled the opportunities for using it.

"Meringues haven't got souls," said Eleanor's mother.

"It's a mercy that they haven't," said Bertie van Tahn; "they would be always losing them, and people like my aunt would get up missions to meringues, and say it was wonderful how much one could teach them and how much more one could learn from them."

"What could you learn from a meringue?" asked Eleanor's mother.

"My aunt has been known to learn humility from an ex-Viceroy,"[4] said Bertie.

"I wish cook would learn to make curry, or have the sense to leave it alone," said Arlington, suddenly and savagely.

Eleanor's face softened. It was like one of his old remarks in the days when there was no abyss between them.

It was during the debate on the Foreign Office vote that Stringham made his great remark that "the people of Crete unfortunately make more history than they can consume locally." It was not brilliant, but it came in the middle of a dull speech, and the House was quite pleased with it. Old gentlemen with bad memories said it reminded them of Disraeli.

It was Eleanor's friend, Gertrude Ilpton, who drew her attention to Arlington's newest outbreak. Eleanor in these days avoided the morning papers.

"It's very modern, and I suppose very clever," she observed.

"Of course it's clever," said Gertrude; "all Lady Isobel's sayings are clever, and luckily they bear repeating."

"Are you sure it's one of her sayings?" asked Eleanor.

"My dear, I've heard her say it dozens of times."

"So that is where he gets his humour," said Eleanor slowly, and the hard lines deepened round her mouth.

The death of Eleanor Stringham from an overdose of chloral,[5] occurring at the end of a rather uneventful season, excited a certain amount of unobtrusive speculation. Bertie van Tahn, who perhaps exaggerated the importance of curry in the home, hinted at domestic sorrow.

And of course Arlington never knew. It was the tragedy of his life that he should miss the fullest effect of his jesting.

---

4   Referring to Lord Curzon of Kedleston, Conservative politician, who served as Viceroy of India from 1899 to 1905. Curzon's public image was of an arrogant and conceited person.

5   Once widely used as a sleeping-aid.

Adrian

A Chapter in Acclimatisation

Westminster Gazette, 9 July 1910, p. 3

His baptismal register spoke of him pessimistically as John Henry, but he had left that behind with the other maladies of infancy, and his friends knew him under the front-name of Adrian. His mother lived in Bethnal Green,[1] which was not altogether his fault; one can discourage too much history in one's family, but one cannot always prevent geography. And, after all, the Bethnal Green habit has this virtue—that it is seldom transmitted to the next generation. Adrian lived in a roomlet which came under the auspicious constellation of W.[2]

How he lived was to a great extent a mystery even to himself; his struggle for existence probably coincided in many material details with the rather dramatic accounts he gave of it to sympathetic acquaintances. All that is definitely known is that he now and then emerged from the struggle to dine at the Ritz or Carlton, correctly garbed and with a correctly critical appetite. On these occasions he was usually the guest of Lucas Croyden, an amiable worldling, who had three thousand a year and a taste for introducing impossible people to irreproachable cookery. Like most men who combine three thousand a year with an uncertain digestion, Lucas was a Socialist, and he argued that you cannot hope to elevate the masses until you have brought plovers' eggs into their lives and taught them to appreciate the difference between coupe

---

1   Area in the East End of London notorious for its slums.
2   The postcode letter stands for 'West': the more desirable part of London.

Jacques and Macédoine de fruits.³ His friends pointed out that it was a doubtful kindness to initiate a boy from behind a drapery counter into the blessedness of the higher catering, to which Lucas invariably replied that all kindnesses were doubtful. Which was perhaps true.

It was after one of his Adrian evenings that Lucas met his aunt, Mrs. Mebberley, at a fashionable tea-shop, where the lamp of family life is still kept burning and you meet relatives who might otherwise have slipped your memory.

"Who was that good-looking boy who was dining with you last night?" she asked. "He looked much too nice to be thrown away upon you."

Susan Mebberley was a charming woman, but she was also an aunt.

"Who are his people?" she continued, when the protégé's name (revised version) had been given her.

"His mother lives at Beth—"

Lucas checked himself on the threshold of what was perhaps a social indiscretion.

"Beth? Where is it? It sounds like Asia Minor. Is she mixed up with Consular⁴ people?"

"Oh, no. Her work lies among the poor."

This was a side-slip into truth. The mother of Adrian was employed in a laundry.

"I see," said Mrs. Mebberley, "mission work of some sort. And meanwhile the boy has no one to look after him. It's obviously my duty to see that he doesn't come to harm. Bring him to call on me."

"My dear Aunt Susan," expostulated Lucas, "I really know very little about him. He may not be at all nice, you know, on further acquaintance."

"He has delightful hair and a weak mouth. I shall take him with me to Homburg⁵ or Cairo."

"It's the maddest thing I ever heard of," said Lucas angrily.

"Well, there is a strong strain of madness in our family. If you haven't noticed it yourself all your friends must have."

"One is so dreadfully under everybody's eyes at Homburg. At least

---

3   Respectively, a sort of fruit sundae with liqueur and a fruit salad.
4   Capitalised in the original.
5   Presumably Bad Homburg, a spa town in Germany favoured by European royalty.

you might give him a preliminary trial at Etretat."⁶

"And be surrounded by Americans trying to talk French? No, thank you. I love Americans, but not when they try to talk French. What a blessing it is that they never try to talk English. Tomorrow at five you can bring your young friend to call on me."

And Lucas, realising that Susan Mebberley was a woman as well as an aunt, saw that she would have to be allowed to have her own way.

Adrian was duly carried abroad under the Mebberley wing; but as a reluctant concession to sanity Homburg and other inconveniently fashionable resorts were given a wide berth, and the Mebberley establishment planted itself down in the best hotel at Dohledorf,⁷ an Alpine townlet somewhere at the back of the Engadine.⁸ It was the usual kind of resort, with the usual type of visitors, that one finds over the greater part of Switzerland during the summer season, but to Adrian it was all unusual. The mountain air, the certainty of regular and abundant meals, and in particular the social atmosphere, affected him much as the indiscriminating fervour of a forcing-house might affect a weed that had strayed within its limits. He had been brought up in a world where breakages were regarded as crimes and expiated as such; it was something new and altogether exhilarating to find that you were considered rather amusing if you smashed things in the right manner and at the recognised hours. Susan Mebberley had expressed the intention of showing Adrian a bit of the world; the particular bit of the world represented by Dohledorf began to be shown a good deal of Adrian.

Lucas got occasional glimpses of the Alpine sojourn, not from his aunt or Adrian, but from the industrious pen of Ida Fisher, a lady who had been at school with Susan Mebberley, and who seemed to have chaperoned her ever since.

"The entertainment which Susan got up last night ended in disaster. I thought it would. The Grobmayer child, a particularly loathsome five-year-old, had appeared as 'Bubbles'⁹ during the early part of the evening,

---

6   Sea resort on the northern French coast.
7   The name is made up, but "-dorf" means "village" in German. "Dohlen" are European jackdaws.
8   Alpine valley in south-eastern Switzerland.
9   The child from the famous Pears soap advertisement, based on a painting originally

and been put to bed during the interval. Adrian watched his opportunity and kidnapped it when the nurse was downstairs, and introduced it during the second half of the entertainment, thinly disguised as a performing pig. It certainly *looked* very like a pig, and grunted and slobbered just like the real article; no one knew exactly what it was, but everyone said it was awfully clever, especially the Grobmayers. At the third curtain Adrian pinched it too hard, and it yelled 'Marmar'! I am supposed to be good at descriptions, but don't ask me to describe the sayings and doings of the Grobmayers at that moment; it was like one of the angrier Psalms set to Strauss's music.[10] We have moved to an hotel higher up the valley."

Miss Fisher's next letter arrived five days later, and was written from the Hotel Steinbock.

"We left the Hotel Victoria this morning. It was fairly comfortable and quiet—at least there was an air of repose about it when we arrived. Before we had been in residence twenty-four hours most of the repose had vanished 'like a dutiful bream,'[11] as Adrian expressed it. However, nothing unduly outrageous happened till last night, when Adrian had a fit of insomnia and amused himself by unscrewing and transposing all the bedroom numbers on his floor. He transferred the bathroom label to the adjoining bedroom door, which happened to be that of Frau Hofrath Schilling,[12] and this morning from seven o'clock onwards the old lady had a stream of involuntary visitors; she was too horrified and scandalised it seems to get up and lock her door. The would-be bathers flew back in confusion to their rooms, and, of course, the change of numbers led them astray again, and the corridor gradually filled with panic-stricken, scantily robed humans, dashing wildly about like rabbits in a ferret-infested warren. It took nearly an hour before the guests were all sorted into their respective rooms, and the Frau Hofrath's condition was still causing some anxiety when we left. Susan is beginning to look

---

      titled 'A Child's World' by Sir John Everett Millais (1829–96).

10 Strauss here could be Johann Strauss I (1804–1849) or one of his sons, Johann II (1825–99), Josef (1827–70) and Eduard (1835–1916). The Austrian family dominated the light music scene and were especially famous for their waltzes.

11 Alluding to the line "Thou art gone from my gaze like a beautiful dream" in the song of that name (also known as 'Spirit of Love') by George Linley (1797–1865).

12 Her title ("Frau Hofrath") indicates high social status; her husband was most likely a high-ranking civil servant in either the German or Austrian civil service.

a little worried. She can't very well turn the boy adrift, as he hasn't got any money, and she can't send him to his people as she doesn't know where they are. Adrian says his mother moves about a good deal and he's lost her address. Probably, if the truth were known, he's had a row at home. So many boys nowadays seem to think that quarrelling with one's family is a recognised occupation."

Lucas's next communication from the travellers took the form of a telegram from Mrs. Mebberley herself. It was sent "reply prepaid," and consisted of a single sentence: "In Heaven's name, where is Beth?"

The Chaplet

A Tragedy of Music at Mealtimes

The Bystander, 15 March 1911, pp. 547–48

It was a gala evening at the Grand Sybaris Hotel, and a special dinner was being served in the Amethyst dining-hall. The Amethyst dining-hall had almost a European reputation, especially with that section of Europe which is historically identified with the Jordan Valley. Its cooking was beyond reproach, and its orchestra was sufficiently highly salaried to be above criticism. Thither came in shoals the intensely musical and the almost intensely musical, who are very many, and in still greater numbers the merely musical, who know how Tchaikowsky's name is pronounced and can recognise several of Chopin's nocturnes if you give them due warning; these eat in the nervous, detached manner of roebuck feeding in the open, and keep anxious ears cocked towards the orchestra for the first hint of a recognisable melody.

"Ah, yes, *Pagliacci*,"[1] they murmur, as the opening strains follow hot upon the soup, and if no contradiction is forthcoming from any better-informed quarter they break forth into subdued humming by way of supplementing the efforts of the musicians. Sometimes the melody starts on level terms with the soup, in which case the banqueters contrive somehow to hum between the spoonfuls; the facial expression of enthusiasts who are punctuating *potage St. Germain with Pagliacci* is not beautiful, but it should be seen by those who are bent on observing

---

1   Italian opera, premiered 1892, by Ruggero Leoncavallo (1857–1919). It was an immediate success with the public despite mixed reviews from critics. The UK premiere took place the following year at the Royal Opera House, Covent Garden.

all sides of life. One cannot discount the unpleasant things of this world merely by looking the other way.

In addition to the aforementioned types the restaurant was patronised by a fair sprinkling of the absolutely non-musical; their presence in the dining-hall could only be explained on the supposition that they had come there to dine.

The earlier stages of the dinner had worn off. The wine lists had been consulted, by some with the blank embarrassment of a schoolboy suddenly called on to locate a Minor Prophet in the tangled hinterland of the Old Testament, by others with the severe scrutiny which suggests that they have visited most of the higher-priced wines in their own homes and probed their family weaknesses. The diners who chose their wine in the latter fashion always gave their orders in a penetrating voice, with a plentiful garnishing of stage directions. By insisting on having your bottle pointing to the north when the cork is being drawn, and calling the waiter Max, you may induce an impression on your guests which hours of laboured boasting might be powerless to achieve. For this purpose, however, the guests must be chosen as carefully as the wine.

Standing aside from the revellers in the shadow of a massive pillar was an interested spectator who was assuredly of the feast, and yet not in it. Monsieur Aristide Saucourt was the *chef* of the Grand Sybaris Hotel, and if he had an equal in his profession he had never acknowledged the fact. In his own domain he was a potentate, hedged around with the cold brutality that Genius expects rather than excuses in her children; he never forgave, and those who served him were careful that there should be little to forgive. In the outer world, the world which devoured his creations, he was an influence; how profound or how shallow an influence he never attempted to guess. It is the penalty and the safeguard of genius that it computes itself by troy weight[2] in a world that measures by vulgar hundredweights.

Once in a way the great man would be seized with a desire to watch the effect of his master-efforts, just as the guiding brain of Krupp's[3] might wish at a supreme moment to intrude into the firing line of an

---

2   Measure used for precious metals and gemstones.
3   Enormous German metal-processing and armaments company.

artillery duel. And such an occasion was the present. For the first time in the history of the Grand Sybaris Hotel, he was presenting to its guests the dish which he had brought to that pitch of perfection which almost amounts to scandal. *Canetons à la mode d'Amblève*.[4] In thin gilt lettering on the creamy white of the menu how little those words conveyed to the bulk of the imperfectly educated diners. And yet how much specialised effort had been lavished, how much carefully treasured lore had been ungarnered, before those six words could be written. In the Department of Deux-Sèvres[5] ducklings had lived peculiar and beautiful lives and died in the odour of satiety[6] to furnish the main theme of the dish; *champignons*, which even a purist for Saxon English would have hesitated to address as mushrooms, had contributed their languorous atrophied bodies to the garnishing, and a sauce devised in the twilight reign of the Fifteenth Louis[7] had been summoned back from the imperishable past to take its part in the wonderful confection. Thus far had human effort laboured to achieve the desired result; the rest had been left to human genius—the genius of Aristide Saucourt.

And now the moment had arrived for the serving of the great dish, the dish which world-weary Grand Dukes and market-obsessed money magnates counted among their happiest memories. And at the same moment something else happened. The leader of the highly salaried orchestra placed his violin caressingly against his chin, lowered his eyelids, and floated into a sea of melody.

"Hark!" said most of the diners, "he is playing 'The Chaplet.'"[8]

They knew it was "The Chaplet" because they had heard it played at luncheon and afternoon tea, and at supper the night before, and had not had time to forget.

"Yes, he is playing 'The Chaplet,'" they reassured one another. The general voice was unanimous on the subject. The orchestra had already played it eleven times that day, four times by desire and seven times from

---

4 Whether this is a real dish remains unclear. "Canetons" are ducklings. Amblève is a river in Belgium.
5 In mid-western France.
6 Punning on the term "odour of sanctity" (used of saints' bodies).
7 1715–74.
8 A musical "entertainment", with words by Moses Mendes (d. 1758) and music by William Boyce (1711–79), first performed 1749.

force of habit, but the familiar strains were greeted with the rapture due to a revelation. A murmur of much humming rose from half the tables in the room, and some of the more overwrought listeners laid down knife and fork in order to be able to burst in with loud clappings at the earliest permissible moment.

And the *Canetons à la mode d'Amblève?* In stupefied, sickened wonder Aristide watched them grow cold in total neglect, or suffer the almost worse indignity of perfunctory pecking and listless munching while the banqueters lavished their approval and applause on the music-makers. Calves' liver and bacon, with parsley sauce, could hardly have figured more ignominiously in the evening's entertainment. And while the master of culinary art leaned back against the sheltering pillar, choking with a horrible brain-searing rage that could find no outlet for its agony, the orchestra leader was bowing his acknowledgments of the hand-clappings that rose in a storm around him. Turning to his colleagues he nodded the signal for an *encore*. But before the violin had been lifted anew into position there came from the shadow of the pillar an explosive negative.

"Noh! Noh! You do not play thot again!"

The musician turned in furious astonishment. Had he taken warning from the look in the other man's eyes he might have acted differently. But the admiring plaudits were ringing in his ears, and he snarled out sharply, "That is for me to decide."

"Noh! You play thot never again," shouted the *chef*, and the next moment he had flung himself violently upon the loathed being who had supplanted him in the world's esteem. A large metal tureen, filled to the brim with steaming soup, had just been placed on a side table in readiness for a late party of diners; before the waiting staff or the guests had time to realise what was happening, Aristide had dragged his struggling victim up to the table and plunged his head deep down into the almost boiling contents of the tureen. At the further end of the room the diners were still spasmodically applauding in view of an *encore*.

Whether the leader of the orchestra died from drowning by soup, or from the shock to his professional vanity, or was scalded to death, the doctors were never wholly able to agree. Monsieur Aristide Saucourt, who now lives in complete retirement, always inclined to the drowning theory.

Wratislav

Westminster Gazette, 12 March 1910, p. 13

The Gräfin's[1] two elder sons had made deplorable marriages. It was a family habit. The youngest boy, Wratislav,[2] who was the black sheep of a rather greyish family, had as yet made no marriage at all.

"There is certainly this much to be said for viciousness," said the Gräfin, "it keeps boys out of mischief."

"Does it?" asked the Baroness Sophie, not by way of questioning the statement, but with a painstaking effort to talk intelligently. It was the one matter in which she attempted to override the decrees of Providence, which had obviously never intended that she should talk otherwise than inanely.

"I don't know why I shouldn't talk cleverly," she would complain; "my mother was considered a brilliant conversationalist."

"These things have a way of skipping one generation," said the Gräfin.

"That seems so unjust," said Sophie; "one doesn't object to one's mother having outshone one as a clever talker, but I must admit that I should be rather annoyed if my daughters talked brilliantly."

"Well, none of them do," said the Gräfin consolingly.

"I don't know about that," said the Baroness, promptly veering round in defence of her offspring. "Elsa said something quite clever on

---

1   Duchess (German).
2   The name may have been chosen purely because it sounded Middle European, but it may be a hidden reference to the English minor poet Theodore William Graf Wratislaw (1871–1933). He was close to the Aesthetes and Decadents of the 1890s and his oeuvre included a few homoerotic poems. Such a reading would explain the choice of the word "viciousness" (deriving from "vice") to describe Wratislav's behaviour, and allow a more telling reading of the story for those in the know.

Thursday about the Triple Alliance.³ Something about it being like a paper umbrella, that was all right as long as you didn't take it out in the rain. It's not everyone who could say that."

"Everyone has said it; at least everyone that I know. But then I know very few people."

"I don't think you're particularly agreeable today."

"I never am. Haven't you noticed that women with a really perfect profile like mine are seldom even moderately agreeable?"

"I don't think your profile is so perfect as all that," said the Baroness.

"It would be surprising if it wasn't. My mother was one of the most noted classical beauties of her day."

"These things sometimes skip a generation, you know," put in the Baroness, with the breathless haste of one to whom repartee comes as rarely as the finding of a gold-handled umbrella.

"My dear Sophie," said the Gräfin sweetly, "that isn't in the least bit clever; but you do try so hard that I suppose I oughtn't to discourage you. Tell me something: has it ever occurred to you that Elsa would do very well for Wratislav? It's time he married somebody, and why not Elsa?"

"Elsa marry that dreadful boy!" gasped the Baroness.

"Beggars can't be choosers," observed the Gräfin.

"Elsa isn't a beggar!"

"Not financially, or I shouldn't have suggested the match. But she's getting on, you know, and has no pretensions to brains or looks or anything of that sort."

"You seem to forget that she's my daughter."

"That shows my generosity. But, seriously, I don't see what there is against Wratislav. He has no debts—at least, nothing worth speaking about."

"But think of his reputation! If half the things they say about him are true—"

"Probably three-quarters of them are. But what of it? You don't want an archangel for a son-in-law."

---

3   Signed in 1882 between Germany, Austria-Hungary and Italy and promising mutual support in case of war with one of the other Great Powers. Italy's commitment to the agreement was doubted by many (and in the event it reneged on it when the First World War broke out).

"I don't want Wratislav. My poor Elsa would be miserable with him."

"A little misery wouldn't matter very much with her; it would go so well with the way she does her hair, and if she couldn't get on with Wratislav she could always go and do good among the poor."

The Baroness picked up a framed photograph from the table.

"He certainly is very handsome," she said doubtfully; adding even more doubtfully, "I dare say dear Elsa might reform him."

The Gräfin had the presence of mind to laugh in the right key.

* * * * *

Three weeks later the Gräfin bore down upon the Baroness Sophie in a foreign bookseller's shop in the Graben,[4] where she was, possibly, buying books of devotion, though it was the wrong counter for them.

"I've just left the dear children at the Rodenstahls'," was the Gräfin's greeting.

"Were they looking very happy?" asked the Baroness.

"Wratislav was wearing some new English clothes, so, of course, he was quite happy. I overheard him telling Toni a rather amusing story about a nun and a mousetrap, which won't bear repetition. Elsa was telling everyone else a witticism about the Triple Alliance being like a paper umbrella—which seems to bear repetition with Christian fortitude."

"Did they seem much wrapped up in each other?"

"To be candid, Elsa looked as if she were wrapped up in a horse-rug. And why let her wear saffron colour?"

"I always think it goes with her complexion."

"Unfortunately it doesn't. It stays with it. Ugh. Don't forget, you're lunching with me on Thursday."

The Baroness was late for her luncheon engagement the following Thursday.

"Imagine what has happened!" she screamed as she burst into the room.

"Something remarkable, to make you late for a meal," said the Gräfin.

"Elsa has run away with the Rodenstahls' chauffeur!"

---

4   One of the main shopping streets in the centre of Vienna.

"Kolossal!"[5]

"Such a thing as that no one in our family has ever done," gasped the Baroness.

"Perhaps he didn't appeal to them in the same way," suggested the Gräfin judicially.

The Baroness began to feel that she was not getting the astonishment and sympathy to which her catastrophe entitled her.

"At any rate," she snapped, "now she can't marry Wratislav."

"She couldn't in any case," said the Gräfin; "he left suddenly for abroad last night."

"For abroad! Where?"

"For Mexico, I believe."

"Mexico! But what for? Why Mexico?"

"The English have a proverb, 'Conscience makes cowboys of us all.'"

"I didn't know Wratislav had a conscience."

"My dear Sophie, he hasn't. It's other people's consciences that send one abroad in a hurry. Let's go and eat."

---

5   Extraordinary, amazing (German).

Filboid Studge

The Story of a Mouse That Helped

The Bystander, 7 December 1910, pp. 483–84

"I want to marry your daughter," said Mark Spayley with faltering eagerness. "I am only an artist with an income of two hundred a year, and she is the daughter of an enormously wealthy man, so I suppose you will think my offer a piece of presumption."

Duncan Dullamy, the great company inflator, showed no outward sign of displeasure. As a matter of fact, he was secretly relieved at the prospect of finding even a two-hundred-a-year husband for his daughter Leonore. A crisis was rapidly rushing upon him, from which he knew he would emerge with neither money nor credit; all his recent ventures had fallen flat, and flattest of all had gone the wonderful new breakfast food, Pipenta, on the advertisement of which he had sunk such huge sums. It could scarcely be called a drug in the market;[1] people bought drugs, but no one bought Pipenta.

"Would you marry Leonore if she were a poor man's daughter?" asked the man of phantom wealth.

"Yes," said Mark, wisely avoiding the error of over-much protestation. And to his astonishment Leonore's father not only gave his consent, but suggested a fairly early date for the wedding.

"I wish I could show my gratitude in some way," said Mark with genuine emotion. "I'm afraid it's rather like the mouse proposing to help the lion."[2]

---

1   Idiom meaning something for which there is no demand.
2   Alluding to Aesop's fable 'The Lion and The Mouse'.

"Get people to buy that beastly muck," said Dullamy, nodding savagely at a poster of the despised Pipenta, "and you'll have done more than any of my agents have been able to accomplish."

"It wants a better name," said Mark reflectively, "and something distinctive in the poster line. Anyway, I'll have a shot at it."

Three weeks later the world was advised of the coming of a new breakfast food, heralded under the resounding name of "Filboid Studge." Spayley put forth no pictures of massive babies springing up with fungus-like rapidity under its forcing influence, or of representatives of the leading nations of the world scrambling with fatuous eagerness for its possession. One huge sombre poster depicted the Damned in Hell suffering a new torment from their inability to get at the Filboid Studge which elegant young fiends held in transparent bowls just beyond their reach. The scene was rendered even more gruesome by a subtle suggestion of the features of leading men and women of the day in the portrayal of the Lost Souls; prominent individuals of both political parties, Society hostesses, well-known dramatic authors and novelists, and distinguished aeroplanists[3] were dimly recognizable in that doomed throng; noted lights of the musical-comedy stage flickered wanly in the shades of the Inferno, smiling still from force of habit, but with the fearsome smiling rage of baffled effort. The poster bore no fulsome allusions to the merits of the new breakfast food, but a single grim statement ran in bold letters along its base: "They cannot buy it now."

Spayley had grasped the fact that people will do things from a sense of duty which they would never attempt as a pleasure. There are thousands of respectable middle-class men who, if you found them unexpectedly in a Turkish bath, would explain in all sincerity that a doctor had ordered them to take Turkish baths; if you told them in return that you went there because you liked it, they would stare in pained wonder at the frivolity of your motive. In the same way, whenever a massacre of Armenians is reported from Asia Minor, everyone assumes that it has been carried out "under orders" from somewhere or another;[4]

---

3   Aeroplanes had been invented less than a decade before and the early pioneers of aviation were household names.

4   The Armenians were a poorly treated minority in the Ottoman empire and were the frequent targets of discrimination and attacks which had varying levels of 'official' approval.

no one seems to think that there are people who might *like* to kill their neighbours now and then.

And so it was with the new breakfast food. No one would have eaten Filboid Studge as a pleasure, but the grim austerity of its advertisement drove housewives in shoals to the grocers' shops to clamour for an immediate supply. In small kitchens solemn pig-tailed daughters helped depressed mothers to perform the primitive ritual of its preparation. On the breakfast-tables of cheerless parlours it was partaken of in silence. Once the womenfolk discovered that it was thoroughly unpalatable, their zeal in forcing it on their households knew no bounds. "You haven't eaten your Filboid Studge!" would be screamed at the appetiteless clerk as he hurried wearily from the breakfast-table, and his evening meal would be prefaced by a warmed-up mess which would be explained as "your Filboid Studge that you didn't eat this morning." Those strange fanatics who ostentatiously mortify themselves, inwardly and outwardly, with health biscuits and health garments, battened aggressively on the new food. Earnest, spectacled young men devoured it on the steps of the National Liberal Club. A bishop who did not believe in a future state[5] preached against the poster, and a peer's daughter died from eating too much of the compound. A further advertisement was obtained when an infantry regiment mutinied and shot its officers rather than eat the nauseous mess; fortunately, Lord Birrell of Blatherstone,[6] who was War Minister at the moment, saved the situation by his happy epigram, that "Discipline to be effective must be optional."

Filboid Studge had become a household word, but Dullamy wisely realised that it was not necessarily the last word in breakfast dietary; its supremacy would be challenged as soon as some yet more unpalatable food should be put on the market. There might even be a reaction in favour of something tasty and appetizing, and the Puritan austerity of the moment might be banished from domestic cookery. At an opportune moment, therefore, he sold out his interests in the article which had brought him in colossal wealth at a critical juncture, and placed his financial reputation beyond the reach of cavil. As for Leonore, who was

---

5   Not so implausible: since the nineteenth century there had been much theological debate about what happened to the soul after death.
6   Not a real person, though Munro may have mockingly ennobled Augustine Birrell (1850–1933), a Liberal politician who was Chief Secretary for Ireland at the time.

now an heiress on a far greater scale than ever before, he naturally found her something a vast deal higher in the husband market than a two-hundred-a-year poster-designer.

Mark Spayley was left to console himself with the bitter reflection that 'tis not in mortals to countermand success.[7]

---

7   Adapting Portius, in Joseph Addison's play *Cato* (1713): "'tis not in mortals to command success" (I. 2. 43).

Ministers of Grace[1]

A Seasonable Political Fantaisie

The Bystander, 30 November 1910, pp. 432–34

Although he was scarcely yet out of his teens, the Duke of Scaw was already marked out as a personality widely differing from others of his caste and period. Not in externals; therein he conformed correctly to type. His hair was faintly reminiscent of Houbigant,[2] and at the other end of him his shoes exhaled the right soupçon of harness-room; his socks compelled one's attention without losing one's respect; and his attitude in repose had just that suggestion of Whistler's mother, so becoming in the really young.[3] It was within that the trouble lay, if trouble it could be accounted, which marked him apart from his fellows. The Duke was religious. Not in any of the ordinary senses of the word; he took small heed of High Church[4] or Evangelical standpoints, he stood outside of all the movements and missions and cults and crusades of the day, uncaring and uninterested. Yet in a mystical-practical way of his own, which had served him unscathed and unshaken through the fickle years of boyhood, he was intensely and intensively religious. His family were naturally, though unobtrusively, distressed about it. "I am so afraid

---

1 Punning on *Hamlet*, I. 4. 39: "Angels and ministers of grace defend us!"
2 French perfume. The House of Houbigant supplied many of the European royal families.
3 Painting of an elderly woman in profile, officially titled "Arrangement in Grey and Black No. 1". The sitter was the mother of the painter, James McNeill Whistler (1834–1903), hence the portrait's nickname.
4 The "High Church" in Anglicanism was the grouping closer in terms of ritual and doctrine to the Roman Catholic Church.

it may affect his bridge," said his mother.

The Duke sat in a pennyworth of chair in St. James's Park,[5] listening to the pessimisms of Belturbet, who reviewed the existing political situation from the gloomiest of standpoints.

"Where I think you political spade-workers are so silly," said the Duke, "is in the misdirection of your efforts. You spend thousands of pounds of money, and Heaven knows how much dynamic force of brain power and personal energy, in trying to elect or displace this or that man, whereas you could gain your ends so much more simply by making use of the men as you find them. If they don't suit your purpose as they are, transform them into something more satisfactory."

"Do you refer to hypnotic suggestion?" asked Belturbet, with the air of one who is being trifled with.

"Nothing of the sort. Do you understand what I mean by the verb to koepenick?[6] That is to say, to replace an authority by a spurious imitation that would carry just as much weight for the moment as the displaced original; the advantage, of course, being that the koepenick replica would do what you wanted, whereas the original does what seems best in its own eyes."

"I suppose every public man has a double, if not two or three," said Belturbet; "but it would be a pretty hard task to koepenick a whole bunch of them and keep the originals out of the way."

"There have been instances in European history of successful koepenickery," said the Duke.

"Oh, there have been False Dimitris and Perkin Warbecks who imposed on the world for a time, but they personated people who were safely dead.[7] It would be far easier to pass oneself off as dead Hannibal[8]

---

5   Park in central London (Westminster), close to Buckingham Palace. You can still hire deckchairs there.

6   Referring to the story of the "Captain of Köpenick": in 1906 a German con man dressed up as a Prussian army officer and ordered a number of real soldiers to help him 'confiscate' 4000 marks from the town hall of Köpenick (east of Berlin).

7   There were three False Dimitris, all of whom claimed to be Ivan the Terrible's youngest son, tsarevich Dmitry Ivanovich, who was otherwise thought dead, possibly assassinated (1582–91). Perkin Warbeck (c. 1474–99) claimed to be Richard of Shrewsbury, Duke of York (the younger of the "Princes in the Tower" whose convenient disappearance allowed their uncle to ascend the throne as Richard III). Warbeck led several small military insurrections to wrest the crown from Henry VII.

8   Carthaginian general who fought the Roman Empire (247–181 B.C. at the latest).

than as living Haldane,⁹ for instance."

"I was thinking," said the Duke, "of the most famous case of all, the angel who koepenicked King Robert of Sicily.¹⁰ Imagine what an advantage it would be to have angels deputising, to use a horrible word, for Lloyd George and F. E. Smith, for instance.¹¹ Then one could dispense with the bother of these recurring General Elections."

"Angels don't exist nowadays; at least, not in that way," said Belturbet; "so what's the good of talking nonsense."¹²

"If you talk to me like that I shall just do it," said the Duke; "it's not everyone who would know how to bring it off, but—"

"Oh, stop that rubbish," said Belturbet, angrily. "Here's Winston coming," he added as a well-known figure approached hurriedly along the almost deserted path.¹³

"Hurry along, dear man," said the Duke to the Minister, who had given him a condescending nod; "your time is short," he continued in a provocative strain. "The whole inept crowd of you will shortly be swept away into the world's waste-paper basket."

"You silly little strawberry-leafed nonentity,"¹⁴ said the Minister, checking himself for a moment in his stride; "the voting masses are on our side; no power of earth or Heaven is going to move us from our place till we choose to quit it."

And Belturbet saw, with bulging eyes, a sudden void, where a moment earlier had been Winston Churchill; a void emphasised rather than relieved by the presence of a puffed-out, bewildered-looking sparrow, which presently fell to a violent cheeping and scolding.

---

9 Presumably Richard Haldane, 1st Viscount Haldane, (1856–1928) Liberal and later Labour politician, Secretary of State for War 1905–12, Lord Chancellor 1912–15.

10 *Tales of a Wayside Inn* (1863) by American poet Henry Wadsworth Longfellow (1807–82) includes the tale of King Robert of Sicily, in which the arrogant king falls asleep in church and awakes to find an angel doppelgänger has taken his place on the throne. Eventually, he is restored, chastened and humbled, to his original status.

11 David Lloyd George (1863–1945), Welsh radical Liberal M.P., at the time Chancellor of the Exchequer (later to become Prime Minister); Frederick Edwin Smith (1872–1930), prominent Conservative M.P.

12 It is a full stop, not a question mark, in the original.

13 Winston Leonard Spencer Churchill (1874–1965), later a Conservative prime minister, but at the time one of the Liberal government's young radicals. He was Home Secretary when this story was written.

14 Strawberry leaves symbolise a duke.

"If we could understand sparrow-language," said the Duke serenely, "I fancy we should hear something infinitely worse than 'strawberry-leafed nonentity.'"

"Good Heavens, Eugène," said Belturbet hoarsely, "what has become of—Why, there he is!"

And he pointed wildly towards a semblance of the vanished Minister, which approached once more along the unfrequented path.

"That, I think you will find, is his angel under-study," said the Duke composedly.

"How beastly happy you two look sitting there," said the Angel-Churchill wistfully.

"I don't suppose you'd care to change places with poor little us," replied the Duke, chaffingly.

"How about poor little me?" said the Angel, modestly. "I've got to run about behind the wheels of popularity, like a spotted dog behind a carriage, getting all the dust and trying to look as if I was an important part of the machine. I must seem a perfect fool to you onlookers sometimes."

"I think you are a perfect angel," said the Duke.

The Angel-that-had-been-Winston smiled, and passed on his way, pursued across the breadth of the Horse Guards' Parade[15] by a tiresome little sparrow that cheeped incessantly and furiously at him.

"That's only the beginning," said the Duke complacently; "I've made it operative with all of them, irrespective of parties."

Belturbet was engaged in feeling his pulse. The Duke fixed his attention on a black swan that was swimming with haughty, stiff-necked aloofness amid the crowd of lesser water-fowl that dotted the ornamental water. For all its pride of mien, something was evidently ruffling and enraging it; in its way it seemed as angry and amazed as the sparrow had been.

At the same moment a human figure came along the pathway.

"Curzon," said Belturbet briefly.

"An Angel-Curzon, if I am not mistaken," said the Duke. "See, he is talking affably to a human being.[16] That settles it."

---

15 A large courtyard, east of St. James' Park, used for the annual 'Trooping the Colour' military parade.
16 See p.40, note 4.

A shabby lounger had accosted the ex-Viceroy. "Could you tell me, sir, if them white birds is storks or halbatrosses? I had an argyment—"

"Those are pelicans. Are you interested in birds? If you would join me in a bun and a glass of milk at the stall yonder I could tell you some interesting things about Indian birds. The hill-mynah, for instance."

The two men disappeared in the direction of the bun-stall, shadowed from the other side of the railed enclosure by a black swan, whose temper seemed to have reached the limit of inarticulate rage.

"I think a prairie oyster[17] on the top of a stiffish brandy-and-soda might save my reason," said Belturbet weakly, as he limped towards his club.

It was late that afternoon before Belturbet could steady his nerves sufficiently to read the evening papers. The Parliamentary report was not reassuring. "Mr. Lloyd George, whose manner was entirely different from either the aggressive or the suave types to which he has accustomed the House, rose to express regret at having, in the course of his speech at Houndsditch[18] the previous night, alluded to certain protesting taxpayers as 'fuddled skulkers.'[19] He realised on reflection that they were probably perfectly honest in their inability to understand certain legal technicalities." (Sensation and some cheers.) Belturbet hurriedly skimmed over a further item of news, "Wild cat found in an exhausted condition in Palace Yard," and ordered another prairie-oyster.

The events of the next few days were piquantly bewildering to the world at large; to Belturbet, who knew dimly what was happening, the situation was fraught with recurring alarms. The young Duke of Scaw, on the other hand, retained all his usual composure. Belturbet, after fruitlessly ringing him up at intervals during the week, ran him to earth one afternoon at his club, smooth and spruce and unruffled as ever. He was reading with evident pleasure a poem in the *English Review*[20] by the Angel-Lady Cardigan,[21] entitled "Pure Women and Clean Men: A

---

17   Drink made of raw egg, Worcestershire sauce, vinegar, salt, and ground black pepper, believed to cure hangovers.
18   Street within the City of London; also part of the East End.
19   Lloyd George did not shy away from attacking opponents of his radical financial plans in vivid terms.
20   Founded in 1908 by Ford Madox Hueffer (later Ford Madox Ford) to publish modern writing.
21   See p. 28, note 9.

Tribute to the Victorian Era." It had attracted much notice, alike for the excellence of its metre and the generosity of its judgments.

"Tell me, what on earth *have* you turned Hensley Henson[22] into?" asked Belturbet anxiously. "I don't fancy he *believes* in angels, and if he finds an angel preaching orthodox sermons from his pulpit while he's been turned into a fox-terrier, he'll develop rabies in less than no time."

"I rather think it was a fox-terrier," said the Duke lazily.

Belturbet groaned heavily. "Look here, Eugène," he cried, "you've got to stop it. Consols[23] are jumping up and down like bronchos."

"Well, you see, the Angel-Balfour's threat to bring eighty thousand Tory stalwarts up to wreck the House[24] unless the Navy Estimates[25] were revised on a Two-Power basis[26] before Parliament was dissolved has created a bit of a sensation. That was really rather a fine passage when he said, 'I glory in the name of Apache.'[27] I wonder, by the way, why the angel up at Dalmeny[28] isn't giving tongue in his support. If there ever was a moment for an epoch-making speech, it's now."

"I saw on the tape this morning that Rosebery refused to address a meeting on the subject. He said something more than mere speech-making was wanted."[29]

---

22 Herbert Hensley Henson (1863–1947), vicar at St. Margaret's Westminster and canon of Westminster Abbey. He published many books and expressed a controversial liberal theology.

23 Government bonds.

24 As Arthur Balfour (British Conservative politician, Prime Minister 1902–05, at the time Leader of the Opposition) actually mobilised Tory peers to come to the House of Lords to thwart the Liberal government's plans to introduce basic social security payments.

25 Proposed budget for financing the Royal Navy.

26 The two-power standard was a defence doctrine that Britain's navy should always be at least as strong as its next two largest rivals combined. It was enacted into law in 1889 as the Naval Defence Act, but by the Edwardian era it had begun to be criticised as overly expensive and inappropriate. (Britain now had only one serious rival: Germany.) In 1909, to the government's consternation, the Admiralty had demanded an increase in the Naval Estimates to finance the building of six new ships of the state-of-the-art 'Dreadnought' type.

27 Name given to delinquent youths in Paris at that time. Munro is parodying George III's utterance "Born and educated in this country, I glory in the name of Briton".

28 In Scotland, the ancestral home of the Earl of Rosebery (1847–1929), Liberal politician and Prime Minister 1894–95.

29 Rosebery was a noted orator; in addition, he could not refrain from criticising the party he had once led.

The young Duke said nothing, but his eyes shone with quiet exultation. Suddenly there was a magnetic stampede of members towards the lobby, where the tape-machines were ticking out some news of more than ordinary import.

"*Coup d'état* in the North. Rosebery seizes Edinburgh Castle."

In the Babel which ensued Belturbet lost sight of his young friend. For the best part of the afternoon he searched one likely haunt after another, spurred on by the sensational posters which the evening papers were displaying broadcast over the West End. "Premier's constituency of East Fife **harried by** Moss-troopers,"[30] was one of the gravest items of news, followed, however, after a brief interval by the reassuring statement: "Government **gives way. Important expansion of naval programme."**

Belturbet gave up his quest, and turned **homeward through St. James's** Park. In **spite of the political ferment which reigned in the** streets **quite a large crowd had gathered to watch the unfolding of a tragedy that had taken place on the shore of the ornamental water. A large black** swan had savagely **attacked a young gentleman who was walking by the water's edge, dragged him down under the surface, and drowned** him. **At the moment when Belturbet arrived on the spot several park-keepers were engaged in lifting the corpse into a punt. Belturbet stooped to pick up a hat that lay near the scene of the struggle. It was a smart soft felt hat, faintly reminiscent of Houbigant.**

Nearly a month elapsed before Belturbet had recovered from his nervous attack sufficiently **to take an interest once more in what was going on** around him. The General Election was **in full** swing. **He called for a batch of morning** papers, and **skimmed through some speeches of the** Lord-Advocate, Mr. F. E. Smith, and other public men, **and then sank back in his chair with a sigh of relief. Evidently the spell had** cease[31] **to act after the** catastrophe **which had overtaken its invoker. There was no trace of angel anywhere.**

---

30   Brigands (historically, those operating around the border between England and Scotland in the seventeenth century).
31   Misprint in the original for "ceased".

Mrs. Pendercoet's Lost Identity

A Tragedy of the Chelsea Arts Club Ball[1]

The Odd Volume 1911, pp. 20–21

Regularly once a year, somewhere about the first week in February,[2] Mrs. Pendercoet was wont to apply to her friends and acquaintances for a character. Not the sort of character which guarantees an applicant for a post of responsibility to be clean and honest and a lifelong abstainer, but a borrowed masquerade identity under which the wearer could momentarily lay aside the matronly state of Pendercoet, solemnly assumed many years ago at St. George's, Hanover Square,[3] and become, if she so willed it, a nautch girl or the Second Mrs. Tanqueray.[4]

"Do suggest some costume for me to go to the Arts' Club Ball in," she would entreat every one; "not Marie Stuart or Diane de Poitiers.[5] Something new and original."

No one had ever suggested that Mrs. Pendercoet should disguise herself as either of these renowned beauties, but she chose to regard the

---

1. Private members' club established in 1891. Chelsea was the centre of artistic bohemia in late nineteenth century London. The club's fancy dress balls (held first at Vestry Hall in the King's Road, then the Royal Opera House in Covent Garden in 1908 and 1909, and from 1910 the Royal Albert Hall) were lavish and correspondingly famous.
2. The balls were held either at New Year or Mardi Gras.
3. Anglican church in central London, a popular location for high society weddings.
4. Respectively, an Indian dancing girl and the title of a controversial but highly successful play by Sir Arthur Wing Pinero (1855–1934), first performed in 1893. Both characters would have been slightly shocking to contemporary conventional morality.
5. Marie (or Mary), Stuart, Queen of Scots (1542–87, ruled 1542–67); Diane de Poitiers (1500–1566), French noblewoman and mistress of King Henri II of France.

proposal as imminent on every one's lips.

"You might go as Liberty," said the Artist.

"Do you mean the shop[6] or the thing in New York Harbour?" said the lady. "I don't think that would suit my style. Too massive. Now I had thought of the Queen of the Butterflies."[7]

"So good of you to think of others," interrupted Rollo.

Rollo was eighteen, and respect for Mrs. Pendercoet was not one of his most marked characteristics.

"I asked for advice, not flippancy," she protested.

"Well, why not go as Caesar's Wife, above reproach,[8] you know. You could have a hobble edging[9] of scandalous newspaper paragraphs in a sort of Plimsoll Line[10] round the base of your skirt, and you'd be above it all, you see."

"Might I ask what you are going as?" said Mrs. Pendercoet severely.

"I'm going as 'Peace persuading the German war fleet to take Antipon.'"[11]

The idea took some seconds to grasp.

"I don't see how you can possibly manage that," she objected.

"I can't. That's where the resemblance will come in."

There was an offended silence which the Artist hastened to break.

"Why not go as the Dawn?" he said; "'the Dawn, which always means good-bye.'"[12]

"But I don't want to mean good-bye," protested the lady; "it's hard enough to find one's partners in all that crush, without saying good-bye to them when you've got them."

"An inspiration!" cried Rollo; "there is one character in fiction one hears no end of, but no one has ever seen her represented in portrait or

---

6   Large luxury department store in Great Marlborough Street, in London's West End.
7   Otherwise known as the Queen Alexandra's birdwing, the largest of all butterfly species, discovered in 1906 and named after King Edward VII's wife.
8   Proverbial ("Caesar's wife must be beyond reproach") from Suetonius and Plutarch.
9   A hobble skirt was a short-lived Edwardian fashion trend of a skirt with a hem around the calves tight enough to make walking difficult.
10 Line painted on the side of a ship to indicate how deep it sits in the water when fully loaded.
11 Antipon was a patent medicine for obesity.
12 Quoting from the poem 'Yasmini' by Laurence Hope (pen-name of Adela Florence Nicolson, 1865–1904), published in *Garden of Kama* (1901).

in the flesh. Go as the Aunt of the Gardener. Every one would welcome her as an old friend the moment she came in with the pen of the Admiral and the good pears of the Ambassador.[13] That woman must have been an inveterate kleptomaniac, you know, or else a very advanced Fabian;[14] nothing seems to have been safe from her. The basket of the washerwoman and the small apricot of the child were no more sacred to her than the property of people better able to afford plundering. Do go as the Aunt of the Gardener, Mrs. Pendercoet. I have a great-uncle who is an admiral, and I'm sure he'd be delighted to lend you a pen."

The Artist abandoned further attempts at peace-mongering, and Mrs. Pendercoet momentarily diverted her attention from the pursuit of fictitious personality to a vigorous and unsparing analysis of Rollo's everyday character. To be recommended a comic costume when one wishes to make a legitimate sensation in some queenly guise is sufficiently annoying to produce plain speaking, and the irate lady could think afterwards of few uncomplimentary remarks that she regretted having left unsaid. Her tongue had the field to itself, so to speak, but Rollo wore the air of one who is keeping his reply in cold storage.

*****

"I've settled on Pomona," Mrs. Pendercoet informed her artist friend a few days later.

The announcement sounded like a news item of the Crofter migration movement[15] or an aeroplane descent in the Orkneys. As a matter of fact it indicated that Mrs. Pendercoet purposed going to the Arts' Club Ball in the character of the Roman Goddess of Orchards.

"A dress of some saffrony-green material, you know, and a basket of autumnal fruits. Simple, but dignified and effective."

It was the basket of fruit that gave Rollo his opportunity on the night of the ball. Mrs. Pendercoet spent a long unhappy evening trying to

---

13 Playing on the artificial sentences stereotypically found as translation exercises in beginner's guides to learning French.
14 The Fabian Society was a democratic socialist campaign group; Rollo is mischievously attributing to them the anarchist idea that "property is theft".
15 The Scottish Highlands and Islands were depopulated in the nineteenth century, with the crofters (small tenant famers) moving to more industrialised areas or emigrating entirely, a process that continued in the twentieth century.

identify herself with the Orchard Goddess, but Rollo had been before her, and their large circle of mutual acquaintances greeted her with a universal chorus of delighted recognition:

"The Aunt of the Gardener! But how *clever*. And the good pears of the Ambassador. So original. Do tell us, was it your own idea?"

And so on throughout the evening. The special artist of the *Daily Pierglass*[16] was supping with Rollo that night, and his picture of "the Aunt of the Gardener, carrying the good pears of the Ambassador and the small apricot of the child: a diverting costume in last night's carnival," is one of Mrs. Pendercoet's bitterest memories.

---

16 Invented.

The Optimist

Westminster Gazette, 2 February 1912, p. 3

In the gathering twilight Richard Duncombe rode a tired horse through a seemingly endless succession of fields in what he guessed to be a more or less homeward direction. After the crowd and movement and liveliness of a good day with the hounds there was something still and ghostly about this long, slow ride through a misty world of plough-land, grass-land, and fallow, in which he and his horse seemed to be the only living things. Even when he struck into a road it seemed a deserted highway bordered by long stretches of hedge and coppice, with never a farm-gate or signpost to break its reticence or relieve its sameness. It was with a sense of pleasure that he came suddenly into the glow of lighted windows and drew rein hopefully outside the garden gate of a substantial-sized dwelling. A tall, red-haired girl stood in the doorway of the house, as though keeping watch along what could be seen of the dusky roadway. She returned Duncombe's greeting with a pleasant "Good evening."

"I see you have a stable there," he called out; "do you think you could let me put my horse up there for an hour's rest and give him a little flour and water? He's fairly done up, and I don't think there's an inn within five miles."

"Mother will be delighted," said the girl, and in a few minutes she had helped Duncombe to stable and water his tired animal.

"We are just sitting down to tea," she said shyly, "and mother hopes you will kindly come in and take a cup."

It was not the first time that Duncombe had partaken of pleasant wayside hospitality during homeward rides, and he gladly accepted the invitation. The house was evidently one belonging to fairly comfortable yeoman owners, and its mistress was a kindly faced woman, with quiet, friendly manners, who sat in her parlour at a table well laid out with the furnishing of a substantial middle-class tea. Seated also at the table when Duncombe entered was a red-haired boy of about seventeen, evidently the brother of the girl who had played the part of stable-help.

Duncombe lost no time in transforming himself from a stranger into an agreeable tea-table guest. He was hungry, and paid due attention to the fact, but he found time to talk, to praise, to take interest in the pictures and old china set round the room, and to wait on his hostess when the kettle needed moving from the hob to the table. He was possessed of a lively, sympathetic nature, that easily attuned itself to the company that he happened to be in, and he would have made himself equally at home at a chapel tea-fight[1] or a Montmartre café-chantant.[2] But on this occasion he became suddenly conscious of the disconcerting fact that he was striking a note of liveliness which met with no response. Behind the natural politeness with which his conversational efforts were received there hung an obvious air of constraint and depression. The mother and daughter made a show of eating and drinking which was little more than a pretence, while the boy sat staring at the wall with an untasted cup of tea before him. Duncombe noted that there was no trace of mourning in their clothes, yet there grew on him the presence of fear in the atmosphere, a sense of something instinctively dreaded, as though a corpse were lying somewhere in the house awaiting burial. He put this feeling down as due in some measure to the lonely situation of the house and the long, dark ride by which he had reached it. The road that ran past it might have been a churchyard path for all the sound it gave back.

As this thought crossed his mind its judgment was belied by the round of approaching hoofs and wheels. The occupants of the room seemed to listen with strained attention, as though the occurrence was too rare to pass without due notice. A gig or light cart of some sort drew up at the gate.

"Go to the door, Nan," said the mother quickly to the daughter.

In a minute the girl returned with a short summons:

"Ted."

---

1 Humorous slang for "tea-party".
2 A café with musical entertainment. Montmartre, in Paris, was known for its red-light district.

The boy rose slowly, drank off his tea at a gulp, and followed the girl out of the room. Duncombe was left alone with the mother, who began to re-question him, with nervous preoccupation, as to the details of the day's run. Nan reappeared for a moment and fetched a boy's overcoat and cap from a chair where they had been lying. Evidently Master Ted was being hustled off to some evening work for which he had no great enthusiasm. When the girl next appeared the receding sound of wheels betokened the cart's departure. There was a moment's silence, which seemed to Duncombe's fancy more tense in constraint than any of its forerunners, and then a sudden volubility descended on his hostess. The departure of the sulky boy to his work or evening class seemed to have loosened her tongue. She gave Duncombe an account of her family history and connexions that was almost defiant in its simple pride. She was a woman apparently on the young side of forty, or not much beyond it, and her children were mere boy and girl, yet her sympathies and interests seemed almost entirely with the past. Her father and her husband's father had belonged to the best yeoman class, and evidently had stood high in their neighbours' esteem. Good friends they seemed to have been, though their political creeds placed them locally in the forefront of the opposed party forces; she related with especial pride an incident which had happened when election passions ran high and an unpopular candidate had been threatened with violence by a hostile mob.

"There was no police anywhere near, and it seemed as if he must be roughly handled, when out he came into the crowd, with my father on one side of him and father-in-law on the other, and everyone made way and let them pass. There wasn't anyone would do anything against my father and father-in-law, they were so looked up to and respected. But those times are gone. I'm as comfortable here to-day as I've ever been, but it isn't the times that used to be, when one could hold up one's head and feel that one was somebody. They'll never come back."

Duncombe hastened with ready confidence to give cheerful denial to the good lady's repining.

"I'll wager you are just as much looked up to by your neighbours as you and yours have been," he said; "there may not be so many ways of showing it, but I'm sure the feeling is there all the same, and it's feeling that counts, you know. Then you've got your young people growing up to take their place in the world; they are going to keep up the family reputation. The good old times will never come back for anyone, but one mustn't turn one's back on the good time coming."

With the flow of cheering counsel on his lips Duncombe prepared to take his departure; he would ride on to the market town a few miles away, leave his horse stabled for the night at some hostelry, and get home by train in time for dinner. He would not dream of offending his hosts by offering anything in way of payment for their hospitality, but a graceful act of recognition suggested and commended itself to him.

"A friend of mine has just brought out a book, 'Old Days in Our Country,'" he said; "if you will allow me, I should like to send you a copy as a souvenir of our talk. Only, remember, you must still put your faith in the new days and the young folk. They are going to be worthy of the times that went before."

He rode off into the dusk, carrying with him the image of a woman's wistful face, a little hard and strained in its hunger for bygone things. As he rode he pieced together her history in his mind; the death first of father and father-in-law, then of husband, and the gradual waning of the family's importance in local affairs; the coming to the fore of newer names, the slipping away of old habits of consultation and consideration, the growing up of a proud feeling of neglected merit which in time would stand like a barrier against social intercourse. The young people had not yet arrived at an age of disposition to assert themselves, and the mother lived in the dead past. That was the thing that had given him, the feeling of something dead lying in the house—the unburied past that still lay above-ground.

Duncombe stabled his horse in the town and caught a train just on the point of starting. In one corner of the carriage two market-women were talking volubly about the heaven-knows-what that market-women do talk about; a stolid policeman gazed vacantly out of the window, and a mechanic read with absorbed attention a crumpled newspaper that had come out of his pocket. On the seat exactly opposite Duncombe sat, or, rather, sprawled, the red-haired boy whom he had last seen walking sulkily out of his mother's parlour. Evidently he was going up to some evening class in the neighbouring cathedral town, and from the expression on his face it did not appear that he regarded the expedition with any particular favour. The evening was not a cold one, but he had turned up the collar of his coat about his ears and drawn his cap forward over his eyes. He returned Duncombe's greeting with the embarrassed shyness of his age, and obviously did not desire to be much more conversational than he had been at the tea-table. But Duncombe, whose mind was still dwelling on the little wayside tragedy of fallen greatness that had been disclosed to him, was not going to let such an opportunity for improving the occasion slip through his hands.

"Your mother has been telling me a lot about old days, and how looked-up-to your father and grandfather were," he said in a quiet, friendly voice, "and I have been telling her that she must look to you to keep up the credit of the name, and show yourself worthy of the stock you come from."

He warmed with enthusiasm to the task of rousing the boy's family pride and putting him on his mettle. "You must stand as high in everyone's esteem as they did, and make your mother as proud of her name in the new days as she was in the old days."

Then he stopped in the middle of his friendly homily; the boy was looking at him with the glazed stare of a trapped and helpless animal that sees the hunter approaching. Once again Duncombe experienced the uncomfortable certainty of being face to face with a tragedy whose nature he could not guess at.

The train drew up at a brightly lit platform. The market-women, still in a full flow of chatter, hooked their arms into a wonderful assortment of baskets, and prepared to disentangle themselves and their burdens from the carriage; the mechanic folded his crumpled newspaper into a tight bunch and thrust it into his pocket. The stolid policeman became suddenly alert and stern-visaged.

"Come along," he said to the red-haired boy, and touched him on the arm.

The boy stumbled to his feet and drew his cap still lower over his eyes. Duncombe, with a sick feeling of distress in his heart, as of one who has struck or trampled on some wounded creature, watched the two thread their way through the cruelly observant station crowd, towards the grim prison that reared its long front beyond the station-walls.

The Romance of Business[1]

Daily News and Leader, 19 March 1914, p. 5

"Ring for some more tea," said Margaret Sangrail to her nephew; "Sophie Chabhouse has just been here, and I always give her inferior tea in my most valuable tea service. The fact that she can neither drink the tea nor carry away the tea-cup fills her with acute anguish, which I find much more amusing than filling her with Lapsang Souchong."

"I'm afraid you're not very fond of Cousin Sophie," said Clovis.[2]

"I make it a rule to like my relations," said Margaret; "I remember only their good qualities and forget their birthdays. Still, when a woman is as indecently rich and as incredibly mean and as unpardonably boastful as Sophie is, a little malicious tail-twisting becomes not merely a pleasure but an absolute duty."

"The boasting is certainly rather unendurable," admitted Clovis; "I met her at lunch yesterday at the Cuverings, and she could talk of nothing else but a fur stole she'd just bought, Lake Baikal beaver, cost her seventy guineas after a fortnight's haggling, probably worth a hundred, and so on, all through lunch time."

---

1 See the introduction for the background to this story. When printed, it was prefaced by the following: "Mr. H. H. MUNRO ("Saki") in response to our request for an article on The Romance of Business, has, in his inimitable way, defined that text in the following:"

2 Clovis Sangrail's name is made up of two allusions to early France. Clovis is an old form of Louis, and there were several Clovises who ruled the Franks in the fifth to seventh centuries. The name means "renowned in battle", which Munro's Clovis often is. Christopher Morley, one of Munro's early editors, suggested Clovis was so called "because he was so appallingly frank" (vii). Expanding on this, Sandie Byrne writes: "Munro, a student of medieval European genealogy, would have known the legends and history of the Frankish king Clovis, whose predilection for swift and nasty vengeance and what he considered poetic justice (he split the skull of a soldier who had split a looted vase with an axe) would have appealed to him" (106). Sangrail is the old French for Holy Grail, the mythical cup that Jesus used at the Last Supper and which was the object of quests in Arthurian legends.

"I heard about that stole from about seven different people," said Margaret placidly, "and when Sophie invited herself to tea I knew that she was coming to flaunt it at me. I just telephoned to Multevey & Princk[3] to send me on approval the best thing in Lake Baikal beaver that they had in stock. When Sophie arrived the first thing she saw was the newly unpacked stole hanging over the back of a chair. 'Why!' she exclaimed, 'Lake Baikal beaver! Exactly like my new stole.' 'Exactly like,' I agreed, 'only a bit larger, and if you don't mind my saying so, rather better quality. In fact its[4] rather better than I can afford. They're asking sixty-two guineas for it.' 'Sixty-two!' screamed Sophie, 'why I gave—' 'Sir Hartley Timming, the greatest living authority on furs, was lunching with me to-day,' I said, 'and he put its value at about sixty, and I daresay they'd let me have it for that, but he strongly advised me not to buy Lake Baikal beaver if I wanted to be in the fashion. "Only second-rate chorus girls and Viennese parvenus wear it," he said, "and all the really well-dressed women are going in for the fur of the soda-mink, that comes from the great soda plains of Northern Alaska." "Still," I said, "beaver is a pretty fur and I never bother much about fashion, and if I could get it for sixty I would think about it,"' and before I could say another word Sophie was weeping and raving and begging me to buy her stole off her.[5] She said she had never really fancied it and had bought it against her better judgment, and had seen a soda mink stole that she really hankered after, and couldn't afford to have both. Finally I took pity on her and bought her seventy guinea beaver at my own figure. Altogether I rather enjoyed her visit."

"I thought I knew something about fur," said Clovis, "but I can't say that I ever heard of Alaska soda-mink before."

"There isn't such an animal," said Margaret, "and there isn't such a person as Sir Hartley Timming, and the real price that Multevey and Princk[6] were asking for their stole was ninety guineas. I suppose you think I showed a certain tendency to untruthfulness in my dealings with Sophie?"

"Not at all," said Clovis; "but I think you've brought the Romance of Business to an advanced stage of perfection."

---

3   Invented.
4   Thus in the original.
5   The muddling of single and double quotation marks is reproduced from the original.
6   The inconsistency ("&" vs "and") is in the original.

Further Reading

General Background Reading

Brooks, David, *The Age of Upheaval: Edwardian Politics 1899–1914*, New Frontiers in History, 1st edn (Manchester: Manchester University Press, 1995).

Hattersley, Roy, *The Edwardians* (London: Abacus, 2006).

Hynes, Samuel, *The Edwardian Turn of Mind* (Princeton: Princeton University Press, 1968).

Malcolm, David and Malcolm, Cheryl Alexander, eds, *The British and Irish Short Story Handbook*, Blackwell Literature Handbooks, 1st edn (Malden, Mass.: Wiley-Blackwell, 2012), https://doi.org/10.1002/9781444355239

Other Works by Saki

Saki, *The Collected Short Stories of Saki* (Ware, Hertfordshire: Wordsworth, 1993).

—, *The Complete Short Stories of Saki*, read by Richard Crowest (Corvidae, 2022), https://corvidae.co.uk/audiobooks/saki/

—, *A Shot in the Dark*, ed. by Adam Newell, 1st edn (London: Hesperus Press Ltd, 2006).

—, *The Penguin Complete Saki* (Harmondsworth: Penguin, 1998).

—. Various works, https://www.gutenberg.org/ebooks/author/152/

On Saki and His Stories

Lorene M. Birden, 'Mappining London: Urban Participation in Sakian Satire', *Literary London Journal*, http://www.literarylondon.org/london-journal/march2004/birden.html

Byrne, Sandie, *The Unbearable Saki: The Work of H. H. Munro*, 1st edn (Oxford: Oxford University Press, 2007).

—, 'The Short Stories of Hector Hugh Munro ("Saki")', in *A Companion to the British and Irish Short Story*, ed. by C.A. Malcolm and D. Malcolm (Chichester: Wiley-Blackwell, 2009), https://doi.org/10.1002/9781444304770.ch12

Ditter, Julia, 'Animals and Animality in Saki's Satirical Short Stories', in *Animal Satire*, ed. by Robert McKay and Susan McHugh, Palgrave Studies in Animals and Literature (Cham: Springer International Publishing, 2023), pp. 243–62, https://doi.org/10.1007/978-3-031-24872-6_15

Drake, Robert, 'Saki's Ironic Stories', *Texas Studies in Literature and Language*, 5.3 (1963), 374–88.

Frost, Adam, 'The Letters of H. H. Munro: Unfinished Business', *English Literature in Transition, 1880–1920*, 44.2 (2001), 199–204.

Gaston, Bruce, *The Annotated Saki* (2016–2024), http://www.annotated-saki.info

—, 'Reconstructing the Original *Beasts and Super-Beasts* by "Saki", or How a Short Story Collection Took Shape', *ANQ: A Quarterly Journal of Short Articles, Notes and Reviews*, 34.0 (2021), 1–6, https://doi.org/10.1080/0895769X.2021.1979929

Gibson, Brian, 'Murdering Adulthood: From Child Killers to Boy Soldiers in Saki's Fiction', in *Childhood in Edwardian Fiction: Worlds Enough and Time*, ed. by Adrienne E. Gavin and Andrew F. Humphries (London: Palgrave Macmillan UK, 2009), pp. 208–23, https://doi.org/10.1057/9780230595132_13

—, *Reading Saki: The Fiction of H. H. Munro* (Jefferson, NC: McFarland, 2014).

Hale, Elizabeth, 'Truth and Claw: The Beastly Children and Childlike Beasts of Saki, Beatrix Potter, and Kenneth Grahame', in *Childhood in Edwardian Fiction: Worlds Enough and Time*, ed. by Adrienne E. Gavin and Andrew F. Humphries (London: Palgrave Macmillan UK, 2009), pp. 191–207, https://doi.org/10.1057/9780230595132_12

Hitchens, Christopher, 'Where the Wild Things Are', *The Atlantic* (June 2008), 109–10, 112, https://www.theatlantic.com/magazine/archive/2008/06/where-the-wild-things-are/306796/

Langguth, A. J., *Saki. A Life Of Hector Hugh Munro With Six Short Stories Never Before Collected* (Oxford: Oxford University Press, 1982).

Maxey, Ruth, '"Children Are Given Us to Discourage Our Better Instincts": The Paradoxical Treatment of Children in Saki's Short Fiction', *Journal of the*

Short Story in English. Les Cahiers de La Nouvelle, 45 (2005), 47–62.

Moran, Sean, 'Vengeance Deferred: Children in Selected Short Stories of Saki', *The Grove*, 21 (2015), 117–34, https://doi.org/10.17561/grove.v0i21.1367

Munro, Ethel M., 'Biography of Saki', in *The Square Egg and Other Sketches, with Three Plays*, by "Saki" (H. H. Munro) (London: John Lane, The Bodley Head, 1924), pp. 3–120.

Reynolds, Rothay, 'A Memoir of H. H. Munro', in *The Toys of Peace and other Papers*, by "Saki" (H. H. Munro) (London: John Lane, The Bodley Head, 1919),
pp. xv–xxvii.

Salemi, Joseph S., 'An Asp Lurking in an Apple-Charlotte: Animal Violence in Saki's *The Chronicles of Clovis*', *Studies in Short Fiction*, 26 (1989), 423–30.

Thrane, James R., 'Two New Stories by "Saki" (H. H. Munro)', *Modern Fiction Studies*, 19.2 (1973), 139–44.

Textual Variants

The changes made when the stories were collected in *The Chronicles of Clovis* are set out below in the following manner:

Story name
(Page number) Version as it appears in this edition] Changes made for *The Chronicles of Clovis*

Esmé
(15) the Irrelevant Man] Clovis
(15) the Irrelevant Man] Clovis
(15) the Man] Clovis
(17) persistent,] persistent
(17) dark,] dark
(19) to practically re-stock] practically to re-stock
(19) hyæna-part] hyæna part

Tobermory
(21) Someone] Some one
(22) Bertie van Tahn's] Clovis's
(22) Bertie van Tahn] Clovis
(24) up hill] up-hill
(24) everyone realised] every one realized
(25) people.] people. Clovis had the presence of mind to maintain a composed exterior; privately he was calculating how long it would take to procure a box of fancy mice through the agency of the Exchange and Mart as a species of hush-money.
(27) party;] party,
(27) Melisande] Mélisande
(27) audience music] audience, music
(27) "Punch."] *Punch*.

(27) Bertie van Tahn] Clovis
(27) to-night] tonight
(27) What's-her-name's] Lady What's-her-name's
(28) Bertie van Tahn] Clovis
(28) Bertie van Tahn] Clovis

Mrs Packletide's Tiger
(29) press] Press
(31) Diana.] Diana. She refused to fall in, however, with Clovis's tempting suggestion of a primeval dance party, at which every one should wear the skins of beasts they had recently slain. "I should be in rather a Baby Bunting condition," confessed Clovis, "with a miserable rabbit-skin or two to wrap up in, but then," he added, with a rather malicious glance at Diana's proportions, "my figure is quite as good as that Russian dancing boy's."
(32) everyone] every one
(32) Mebbin] Mebbin,

The Background
(33) Henri] "That woman's art-jargon tires me," said Clovis to his journalist friend. "She's so fond of talking of certain pictures as 'growing on one,' as though they were a sort of fungus."

"That reminds me," said the journalist, "of the story of Henri Deplis. Have I ever told it you?"

Clovis shook his head.

"Henri
(33) It] "It
(33) patronise] patronize
(34) It] "It
(34) tarveller] traveller
(34) But] "But
(35) A] "A
(35) The] "The
(36) Meanwhile] "Meanwhile
(36) In] "In
(36) sane.] sane."

The Jesting Of Arlington Stringham

(37) "it's] "It's
(38) everyone] every one
(38) "By Mere and Wold"] *By Mere And Wold*
(38) "By Mere Chance,"] *By Mere Chance,*
(38) everyone] every one
(39) the odious Bertie van Tahn was] Clovis and the odious Bertie van Tahn were
(39) It] At dinner that night it
(39) Bertie van Tahn] Clovis
(40) Bertie] Clovis
(40) Bertie van Tahn] Clovis

Adrian

(41) Acclimatisation] Acclimatization
(42) tea-shop] teashop
(43) realising] realizing
(43) recognised] recognized
(43) Ida Fisher, a lady who had been at school with Susan Mebberley, and who seemed to have chaperoned her ever since.] Clovis, who was also moving as a satellite in the Mebberley constellation.
(43) everyone] every one
(44) Miss Fisher's] Clovis's
(44) scandalised] scandalized
(44) recognised] recognized

The Chaplet

(47) The Chaplet
A Tragedy Of Music At Mealtimes] The Chaplet
(47) It] A strange stillness hung over the restaurant; it was one of those rare moments when the orchestra was not discoursing the strains of the Ice-cream Sailor waltz.

   "Did I ever tell you," asked Clovis of his friend, "the tragedy of music at mealtimes?"

   "It
(47) recognise] recognize
(47) recognisable] recognizable
(47) "Ah, yes, *Pagliacci*] "'Ah, yes, Pagliacci

(47) *potage St. Germain with Pagliacci*] potage St. Germain with Pagliacci
(48) In] "In
(48) patronised] patronized
(48) The] "The
(48) Standing] "Standing
(48) Once] "Once
(48) *Canetons à la mode d'Amblève*] Canetons à la mode d'Amblève
(48) specialised] specialized
(48) *champignons*] champignons
(49) And] "And
(49) "Hark!"] "'Hark!'"
(49) 'he] 'he
(49) 'The Chaplet.'"] "The Chaplet.'"
(49) They] "They
(49) "The Chaplet"] 'The Chaplet'
(49) "Yes] "'Yes
(49) 'The Chaplet,'"] "The Chaplet,'"
(50) And the *Canetons à la mode d'Amblève?*] "And the Canetons à la mode d'Amblève?
(50) *encore*] encore
(50) "Noh!] "'Noh!
(50) again!"] again!'
(50) The] "The
(50) "That] 'That
(50) decide."] decide.'
(50) "Noh!] "'Noh!
(50) again,"] again,'
(50) realise] realize
(50) *encore*] encore
(50) Whether] "Whether
(50) theory.] theory."

Wratislav
(51) was a] was, observed Clovis, a
(51) everyone] every one
(52) "Everyone] "Every one
(52) everyone] every one

Filboid Studge, The Story of A Mouse That Helped
(55) over-much protestation] over-protestation
(57) Earnest, spectacled] Earnest spectacled
(57) realised] realized
(57) poster-designer.
Mark Spayley was left to console himself with the bitter reflection that 'tis not in mortals to countermand success.] poster designer. Mark Spayley, the brainmouse who had helped the financial lion with such untoward effect, was left to curse the day he produced the wonder-working poster.

"After all," said Clovis, meeting him shortly afterwards at his club, "you have this doubtful consolation, that 'tis not in mortals to countermand success."

Ministers of Grace: A Seasonable Political Fantaisie
(59) Ministers of Grace
A Seasonable Political Fantaisie] "Ministers of Grace"
(60) successful] highly successful
(60) Duke.] Duke dreamily.
(60) "Oh, there] "Oh, of course, there
(60) Warbecks who] Warbecks, who
(60) time, but] time," assented Belturbet, "but
(60) safely dead.] dead or safely out of the way. That was a comparatively simple matter.
(61) Sicily.] Sicily with such brilliant results.
(61) Imagine] Just imagine
(61) deputising] deputizing
(61) horrible] horrible but convenient
(61) Lloyd George and F. E. Smith, for instance. Then one could dispense with the bother of these recurring General Elections."] Quinston and Lord Hugo Sizzle, for example. How much smoother the Parliamentary machine would work than at present!"
(61) "Angels] "Now you're talking nonsense," said Belturbet; "angels
(61) nowadays;] nowadays,
(61) way," said Belturbet; "so what's the good of talking nonsense."] way, so what is the use of dragging them into a serious discussion? It's merely silly."
(61) do] *do*]

(61) Duke; "it's not everyone who would know how to bring it off, but—"] Duke.

"Do what?" asked Belturbet. There were times when his young friend's uncanny remarks rather frightened him.

"I shall summon angelic forces to take over some of the more troublesome personalities of our public life, and I shall send the ousted originals into temporary retirement in suitable animal organisms. It's not every one who would have the knowledge or the power necessary to bring such a thing off—"

(61) that] that inane
(61) Belturbet, angrily. "Here's Winston] Belturbet angrily; "it's getting wearisome. Here's Quinston
(61) added as a well-known figure approached hurriedly along the almost deserted path.] added, as there approached along the almost deserted path the well-known figure of a young Cabinet Minister, whose personality evoked a curious mixture of public interest and unpopularity.
(61) dear] my dear
(61) Duke] young Duke
(61) is] is running
(61) strain. "The] strain; "the
(61) silly] poor
(61) stride; "the] stride and rolling out his words spasmodically; "who is going to sweep us away, I should like to know? The
(61) side; no] side, and all the ability and administrative talent is on our side too. No
(61) it."] it. No power of earth or—"
(61) And Belturbet] Belturbet
(61) void, where] void where
(61) Winston Churchill] a Cabinet Minister
(61) emphasised] emphasized
(61) puffed-out, bewildered-looking] puffed-out bewildered-looking
(61) presently] hopped about for a moment in a dazed fashion and then
(62) "Good] "But good
(62) is!"
And] is! How on earth did he get there?" And

(62) wildly] with a shaking finger
(62) "That, I think you will find, is his angel under-study," said the Duke composedly.] The Duke laughed.

"It is Quinston to all outward appearance," he said composedly, "but I fancy you will find, on closer investigation, that it is an angel understudy of the real article."

The Angel-Quinston greeted them with a friendly smile.

(62) said the Angel-Churchill] he said
(62) Duke,] Duke
(62) Angel,] Angel
(62) Angel-that-had-been-Winston] Angel-that-had-been-Quinston
(62) Guards'] Guards
(62) Belturbet] Belturbet made no coherent reply; he
(62) attention] attention with some interest
(62) mien] bearing
(62) pathway.] pathway. Belturbet looked up apprehensively.
(62) Curzon," said Belturbet] "Kedzon," he whispered
(62) Angel-Curzon] Angel-Kedzon
(62) "See,] "Look,
(63) shabby] shabbily dressed
(63) ex-Viceroy] the man who had been Viceroy in the splendid East, and who still reflected in his mien some of the cold dignity of the Himalayan snow-peaks.
(63) argyment—"
   "Those] argyment—"
The cold dignity thawed at once into genial friendliness.
"Those
(63) pelicans.] pelicans, my dear sir.
(63) yonder I] yonder, I
(63) birds. The hill-mynah, for instance.] birds. Right oh! Now the hill-mynah, for instance—
(63) bun-stall, shadowed] bun stall, chatting volubly as they went, and shadowed
(63) rage.] rage.

Belturbet gazed in an open-mouthed wonder after the retreating couple, then transferred his attention to the infuriated swan, and finally turned with a look of scared comprehension at his young friend lolling unconcernedly in his chair. There was no longer any room to doubt what was happening. The "silly talk" had been translated into terrifying action.

(63) that afternoon before Belturbet] in the day before he

(63) read] glance at

(63) was not reassuring. "Mr. Lloyd George, whose manner was entirely different from either the aggressive or the suave types to which he has accustomed the House, rose to express regret at having, in the course of his speech at Houndsditch the previous night, alluded to certain protesting taxpayers as 'fuddled skulkers.'] proved significant reading, and confirmed the fears that he had been trying to shake off. Mr. Ap Dave, the Chancellor, whose lively controversial style endeared him to his supporters and embittered him, politically speaking, to his opponents, had risen in his place to make an unprovoked apology for having alluded in a recent speech to certain protesting taxpayers as "skulkers."

(63) realised] had realized

(63) probably] in all probability

(63) technicalities." (Sensation and some cheers.)] technicalities of the new finance laws. The House had scarcely recovered from this sensation when Lord Hugo Sizzle caused a further flutter of astonishment by going out of his way to indulge in an outspoken appreciation of the fairness, loyalty, and straightforwardness not only of the Chancellor, but of all the members of the Cabinet. A wit had gravely suggested moving the adjournment of the House in view of the unexpected circumstances that had arisen.

(63) hurriedly] anxiously

(63) news,] news printed immediately below the Parliamentary report:

(63) Yard," and ordered another prairie-oyster.] Yard."

"Now I wonder which of them—" he mused, and then an appalling idea came to him. "Supposing he's put them both into the same beast!" He hurriedly ordered another prairie oyster.

Belturbet was known in his club as a strictly moderate drinker; his consumption of alcoholic stimulants that day gave rise to considerable comment.

(63) alarms. The young Duke of Scaw, on the other hand, retained

all his usual composure. Belturbet, after fruitlessly ringing him up at intervals during the week,] alarms. The old saying that in politics it's the unexpected that always happens received a justification that it had hitherto somewhat lacked, and the epidemic of startling personal changes of front was not wholly confined to the realm of actual politics. The eminent chocolate magnate, Sadbury, whose antipathy to the Turf and everything connected with it was a matter of general knowledge, had evidently been replaced by an Angel-Sadbury, who proceeded to electrify the public by blossoming forth as an owner of race-horses, giving as a reason his matured conviction that the sport was, after all, one which gave healthy open-air recreation to large numbers of people drawn from all classes of the community, and incidentally stimulated the important industry of horse-breeding. His colours, chocolate and cream hoops spangled with pink stars, promised to become as popular as any on the Turf. At the same time, in order to give effect to his condemnation of the evils resulting from the spread of the gambling habit among wage-earning classes, who lived for the most part from hand to mouth, he suppressed all betting news and tipsters' forecasts in the popular evening paper that was under his control. His action received instant recognition and support from the Angel-proprietor of the *Evening Views*, the principal rival evening halfpenny paper, who forthwith issued an ukase decreeing a similar ban on betting news, and in a short while the regular evening Press was purged of all mention of starting prices and probable winners. A considerable drop in the circulation of all these papers was the immediate result, accompanied, of course, by a falling-off in advertisement value, while a crop of special betting broadsheets sprang up to supply the newly-created want. Under their influence the betting habit became if anything rather more widely diffused than before. The Duke had possibly overlooked the futility of koepenicking the leaders of the nation with excellently intentioned angel under-studies, while leaving the mass of the people in its original condition.

Further sensation and dislocation was caused in the Press world by the sudden and dramatic *rapprochement* which took place between the Angel-Editor of the *Scrutator* and the Angel-Editor of the *Anglian Review*, who not only ceased to criticize and disparage the tone and tendencies of each other's publication, but agreed to exchange editorships for alternating periods. Here again public support was not on the side of the angels; constant readers of the *Scrutator* complained bitterly of the strong meat which was thrust upon them at fitful intervals in place of the almost vegetarian diet to which they had become confidently accustomed; even those who were not mentally averse to strong meat as a separate course were pardonably annoyed at being supplied with it in the pages of the *Scrutator*. To be suddenly confronted with a pungent herring salad when one had attuned oneself to tea and toast, or to discover a richly truffled segment of *paté de foi*e dissembled in a bowl of bread and milk, would be an experience that might upset the equanimity of the most placidly disposed mortal. An equally vehement outcry arose from the regular subscribers of the *Anglian Review* who protested against being served from time to time with literary fare which no young person of sixteen could possibly want to devour in secret. To take infinite precautions, they complained, against the juvenile perusal of such eminently innocuous literature was like reading the Riot Act on an uninhabited island. Both reviews suffered a serious falling-off in circulation and influence. Peace hath its devastations as well as war.

The wives of noted public men formed another element of discomfiture which the young Duke had almost entirely left out of his calculations. It is sufficiently embarrassing to keep abreast of the possible wobblings and veerings-round of a human husband, who, from the strength or weakness of his personal character, may leap over or slip through the barriers which divide the parties; for this reason a merciful politician usually marries late in life, when he has definitely made up his mind on which side he wishes his wife to be socially valuable. But these trials were as nothing compared to the bewilderment caused by the Angel-husbands who seemed in some cases to have revolutionized their outlook on life in the interval between breakfast and dinner, without premonition or preparation of any kind, and apparently without realizing the least need for subsequent explanation. The temporary peace which brooded over the Parliamentary situation was by no means reproduced in the home circles of the leading statesmen and politicians. It had been frequently and extensively remarked of Mrs Exe that she would try the patience of an angel; now the tables were reversed, and she unwittingly had an opportunity for discovering that the capacity for exasperating behaviour was not all on one side.

And then, with the introduction of the Navy Estimates, Parliamentary peace suddenly dissolved. It was the old quarrel between Ministers and the Opposition as to the adequacy or the reverse of the Government's naval programme. The Angel-Quinston and the Angel-Hugo-Sizzle contrived to keep the debates free from personalities and pinpricks, but an enormous sensation was created when the elegant lackadaisical Halfan Halfour threatened to bring up fifty thousand stalwarts to wreck the House if the Estimates were not forthwith revised on a Two-Power basis. It was a memorable scene when he rose in his place, in response to the scandalized shouts of his opponents, and thundered forth, "Gentlemen, I glory in the name of Apache."

Belturbet, who had made several fruitless attempts to ring up his young friend since the fateful morning in St. James's Park,

(63) ever. He was reading with evident pleasure a poem in the *English Review* by the Angel-Lady Cardigan, entitled "Pure Women and Clean Men: A Tribute to the Victorian Era." It had attracted much notice, alike for the excellence of its metre and the generosity of its judgments.] ever.

(64) *have*] have

(64) Hensley Henson] Cocksley Coxon

(64) anxiously.] anxiously, mentioning the name of one of the pillars of unorthodoxy in the Anglican Church.

(64) heavily.] heavily, and sank into a chair.

(64) cried,] whispered hoarsely, having first looked well round to see that no one was within hearing range,

(64) bronchos."

"Well, you see, the Angel-Balfour's threat to bring eighty thousand Tory stalwarts up to wreck the House unless the Navy Estimates were revised on a Two-Power basis before Parliament was dissolved has created a bit of a sensation. That was really rather a fine passage when he said, 'I glory in the name of Apache.' I wonder, by the way, why the angel up at Dalmeny isn't giving tongue in his support. If there ever was a moment for an epoch-making speech, it's now."

"I saw] bronchos, and that speech of Halfour's in the House last night has simply startled everybody out of their wits. And then on the top of it, Thistlebery—"

"What has he been saying?" asked the Duke quickly.

"Nothing. That's just what's so disturbing. Every one thought it was

simply inevitable that he should come out with a great epoch-making speech at this juncture, and I've just seen
(64) Rosebery] he has
(64) a meeting on the subject. He said] any meetings at present, giving as a reason his opinion that
(65) exultation. Suddenly] exultation.

"It's so unlike Thistlebery," continued Belturbet; "at least," he said suspiciously, "it's unlike the *real* Thistlebery—"

"The real Thistlebery is flying about somewhere as a vocally-industrious lapwing," said the Duke calmly; "I expect great things of the Angel-Thistlebery," he added.

At this moment
(65) Rosebery] Thistlebery
(65) Castle."] Castle. Threatens civil war unless Government expands naval programme."
(65) Babel] babel
(65) End. "Premier's constituency of East Fife] End. "General Baden-Baden mobilizes Boy-Scouts. Another *coup d'état* feared. Is Windsor Castle safe?" This was one of the earlier posters, and was followed by one of even more sinister purport: "Will the Test-match have to be postponed?" It was this disquietening question which brought home the real seriousness of the situation to the London public, and made people wonder whether one might not pay too high a price for the advantages of party government. Belturbet, questing round in the hope of finding the originator of the trouble, with a vague idea of being able to induce him to restore matters to their normal human footing, came across an elderly club acquaintance who dabbled extensively in some of the more sensitive market securities. He was pale with indignation, and his pallor deepened as a breathless newsboy dashed past with a poster inscribed: "Premier's constituency
(65) Moss-troopers, was one of the gravest items of news, followed, however, after a brief interval by the reassuring statement: "Government] moss-troopers. Halfour sends encouraging telegram to rioters. Letchworth Garden City threatens reprisals. Foreigners taking refuge in Embassies and National Liberal Club."

"This is devils' work!" he said angrily.

Belturbet knew otherwise.

At the bottom of St. James's Street a newspaper motor-cart, which had just come rapidly along Pall Mall, was surrounded by a knot of eagerly talking people, and for the first time that afternoon Belturbet heard expressions of relief and congratulation.
It displayed a placard with the welcome announcement: "Crisis ended. Government

(65) Belturbet gave up his quest, and turned] There seemed to be no immediate necessity for pursuing the quest of the errant Duke, and Belturbet turned to make his way

(65) Park. In] Park. His mind, attuned to the alarums and excursions of the afternoon, became dimly aware that some excitement of a detached nature was going on around him. In

(65) streets] streets,

(65) swan had savagely] swan, which had recently shown signs of a savage and dangerous disposition, had suddenly

(65) him.] him before anyone could come to his assistance.

(65) recovered from his nervous attack sufficiently] sufficiently recovered from his attack of nervous prostration

(65) around him. The General Election was] in the world of politics. The Parliamentary Session was still

(65) swing.] swing, and a General Election was looming in the near future.

(65) papers, and] papers and

(65) Lord-Advocate, Mr. F. E. Smith, and other public men,] Chancellor, Quinston, and other Ministerial leaders, as well as those of the principal Opposition champions,

(65) cease] ceased

(65) catastrophe] tragedy

About the Team

Alessandra Tosi was the managing editor for this book.

Rose Cook proofread this book.

Jeevanjot Kaur Nagpal designed the cover. The cover was produced in InDesign using the Fontin font.

Cameron Craig typeset the book in InDesign and produced the paperback and hardback editions. The text font is Tex Gyre Pagella and the heading font is Californian FB.

Cameron also produced the PDF and HTML editions. The conversion was performed with open-source software and other tools freely available on our GitHub page at https://github.com/OpenBookPublishers.

Jeremy Bowman created the EPUB.

This book has been anonymously peer-reviewed by experts in their field. We thank them for their invaluable help.

This book need not end here...

Share

All our books — including the one you have just read — are free to access online so that students, researchers and members of the public who can't afford a printed edition will have access to the same ideas. This title will be accessed online by hundreds of readers each month across the globe: why not share the link so that someone you know is one of them?

This book and additional content is available at:
https://doi.org/10.11647/OBP.0365

Donate

Open Book Publishers is an award-winning, scholar-led, not-for-profit press making knowledge freely available one book at a time. We don't charge authors to publish with us: instead, our work is supported by our library members and by donations from people who believe that research shouldn't be locked behind paywalls.

Why not join them in freeing knowledge by supporting us:
https://www.openbookpublishers.com/support-us

Follow @OpenBookPublish

Read more at the Open Book Publishers BLOG

You may also be interested in:

The Classic Short Story, 1870–1925
Theory of a Genre
Florence Goyet (author); Yvonne Freccero (translator)

https://doi.org/10.11647/obp.0039

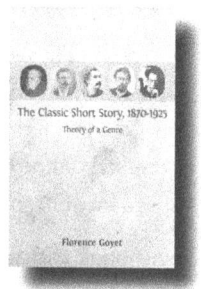

The Life and Letters of William Sharp and "Fiona Macleod"
Volume 1: 1855–1894
William F. Halloran

https://doi.org/10.11647/obp.0142

Prose Fiction
An Introduction to the Semiotics of Narrative
Ignasi Ribó

https://doi.org/10.11647/obp.0187

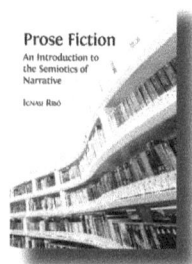

www.ingramcontent.com/pod-product-compliance
Lightning Source LLC
Chambersburg PA
CBHW071121160426

43196CB00013B/2654